AFGHANISTAN

A Russian Soldier's Story

Afghanistan

- ✪ National capital
- • Province capital
- ☒ Airport
- —— International boundary
- ---- Province boundary

0   100   200 km

0   100 mi

©MAGELLAN Geographix℠Santa Barbara, CA (800) 929-4627

AFGHANISTAN

A Russian Soldier's Story

TEXT AND PHOTOGRAPHS BY
Vladislav Tamarov

TRANSLATED BY
Naomi Marcus, Marianne Clarke Trangen, and Vladislav Tamarov

TEN SPEED PRESS
Berkeley

All rights reserved. Published in the United States by Ten Speed Press, an imprint
of the Crown Publishing Group, a division of Random House, Inc., New York.
www.crownpublishing.com
www.tenspeed.com

Ten Speed Press and the Ten Speed Press colophon are registered trademarks of
Random House, Inc.

Originally published as *Afghanistan: Soviet Vietnam* by Mercury House
(San Francisco, California), in 1992.

Library of Congress Cataloging-in-Publication Data is on file with the publisher.

ISBN: 978-1-58008-416-1

Interior design by Ann Flanagan Typography
Interior art direction by Sharon Smith
Cover design by Nancy Austin
Photographs by Vladislav Tamarov

First Ten Speed Press Edition

147030457

Contents

APPLICATION FOR MILITARY SERVICE	
1. Last Name	TAMAROV
2. First Name, Patronymic	Vladislav Evgenievich
3. Date/Place of Birth	January 12, 1965 Leningrad
4. Nationality	Russian
5. Marital Status	Single
6. Party Affiliation	Member of the Komsomols since 1979
7. Profession	Student at Leningrad Pedagogical Institute, Sports Department
8. I agree to serve in the territory of Afghanistan.	YES _X_ No____
9. Date of Application	April 26, 1984

INTRODUCTION

It was my first day at peace. The first day that I didn't hit the dirt at the slightest rustle, that I didn't have to hide in the shade of the trees, holding my gun at the ready. The first day that it was possible to simply walk along the road, not thinking about anything at all, without having to look down all the time to avoid being blown up on a mine. It was the first day I came back from Afghanistan.

I walked out of the airport, sat down on a park bench, and opened my notebook to the last page. Here was my little calendar on which I'd crossed off every completed "Afghan day." Unhurriedly, enjoying this moment, I drew my last—six hundred twenty-first—cross, on April 24, 1986.

When I was drafted into the army in April 1984, I was a nineteen-year-old boy. The club where they took us was a distribution center. Officers came there from various military units and picked out the soldiers they wanted. My fate was decided in one minute. A young officer came up to me and asked, "Do you want to serve in the commandos, the Blue Berets?" Of course I agreed. Two hours later I was on a plane to Uzbekistan (a Soviet republic in Central Asia), where our training base was located.

During the flight, I learned most of the soldiers from this base were sent to Afghanistan. I wasn't scared. I wasn't surprised. At that point I didn't care anymore because I understood that it was impossible to change anything. "To serve in the Soviet army is the honorable duty of Soviet citizens"—as it's written in our Constitution. And no one gives a damn whether you want to fulfill this "honorable duty" or not. But then I didn't know anything about Afghanistan. Up until 1985, in the press and on television, they told us that Soviet soldiers in Afghanistan were planting trees and building schools and hospitals. And only a few knew that more and more cemeteries were being filled with the graves of eighteen- to twenty-year-old boys. Without the dates of their death, without inscriptions. Only their names on black stone...

At the base we were trained and taught to shoot. We were told that we were being sent to Afghanistan not to plant trees. And as to building schools, we simply wouldn't have the time. We were told that *there* we would be defending the southern borders of the Soviet Union, as well as the Afghan revolution.

Three and a half months later, my plane was landing in Kabul, the capital of Afghanistan. When I stepped off the plane, the first thing I did was look for the skyscrapers. (After all, it was a capital city, "abroad.") But instead of skyscrapers, I found only reddish, faded mountains. We were taken to a club on base. A few minutes later, officers started to come by and choose soldiers. Suddenly, an officer with a smiling face and sad eyes burst in noisily. He looked us over with an appraising glance and pointed his finger at me: "Ah ha! I see a minesweeper!" That's how I became a minesweeper. Ten days later, I went on my first combat mission.

Now I'm often asked if I thought the war was a just war when I was there. How can I answer? I was a boy who was born and raised in quiet, beautiful Leningrad, a boy who loved his parents and went obediently to school. A boy who was yanked out of that life and dumped in a strange land where there was a real war going on, where life followed different rules. And the most important rule was simple: only those who kill first will survive. *There*, we didn't have "smart thoughts." We shot at those who were shooting at us; we killed those who were killing us.

In our company there was a board on which were written the names of those who'd perished, and the dates.

During the twenty months I served in Afghanistan, five more names went on the board, three more black days:

APRIL 17, 1985. ALEKSEI KONDRASHEV. 19 [blown up on a mine]

MAY 25, 1985. ALEKSANDR ZAICHENKO. 19 [killed in battle]

JULY 10, 1985. SERGEI ZAITSEV. 19

ALEKSANDR KRAVCHENKO. 19

YURI DEMYANETS. 18

[They were blown up by *one* mine while checking a road.]

They were eighteen and nineteen years old. At home, their mothers were waiting for them, mothers who had given birth to them, who carried them in their arms when they were small, who woke them up to go to school, who couldn't do anything when their sons were taken into the army, who couldn't do anything when—instead of their sons—they were presented with a form: "Your son perished while fulfilling his international duty in Afghanistan."

I wrote this paragraph, and I thought: why did I write it? Simply, it was very painful for me to read these names once more as they were written there.

Now, our troops have returned from Afghanistan.

Now, our government has announced that the war was "a mistake."

Now, I think about the results of this *mistake.* Tens of thousands killed, hundreds of thousands of bodies crippled and fates twisted. That is the only result of this war. What can any war give, aside from such results?

I flew home to my native Leningrad. Only one day separated me from Afghanistan, but it already seemed to me that it had been some kind of terrible dream. I fell asleep with this thought: that when I awoke, the war would remain in my dreams, and it wouldn't haunt me anymore.

When I awoke, the plane was coming in for a landing. Through the window, the lights of my city were visible. The city where I hadn't been for two long, hard years. I had dreamed about this moment for 621 days, that is, for 14,904 hours.

I wanted my homecoming to be a surprise. But right before I reached our

3

street, I became scared for my mom. And I called her up: "Mama! I'm alive, I'm in Leningrad! I'll be right there!" And I hung up. I don't remember what happened when I got home. I couldn't take anything in. I remember only that everyone cried. And when I woke up in the morning, at six o'clock on the dot, and I saw my familiar walls, my cat curled up at my feet, I understood that it was over—that Afghanistan was in my past. And a sharp pain went through my heart—I wanted to bang against the walls, drop everything, and go back. Go back there, where I knew my purpose, where I knew the value of life, where I was needed. To this day, I still have Afghan dreams, from which I awaken in great pain and sadness. But it's too late to go back or to bring anyone back.

I am asked a lot, "Was it terrible for you there?" It's a complicated question. The first year and a half I didn't think about it. I just didn't think. It was more like . . . a curiosity. Bullets whip up little fountains of dirt all around you, a few centimeters away, and you're lying there and all sorts of absurd, silly thoughts keep occurring to you: "Wow, that was close! I've got to write home about that one. Only not to my parents, I'll write my friend." But our casual attitude is not out of bravery or courage. No. It's probably simply that we lived alongside death all the time. And when you live next to death like that, you don't think about it anymore, you just try to encounter it as seldom as possible. I remember when we were ambushed once, I had to jump out from behind a rock and run about thirty-five meters under a hail of bullets. In those moments I didn't think about death—it was just so hard to tear my back away from the cliffs and go. But when there were only six months left for me to serve, then I knew the meaning of fear. You can hear that it's not your bullet, but still you press close to the ground and you're terrified, not just of dying, but it's terrifying to think of dying when you're so close to home.

Some call us heroes, others call us killers. Why? We are the veterans of the Afghan war—Afghantsi. That word says it all. Simply, *there* we had our own life, another life, and we lived it as best as we could. That life was lived by other values, other criteria. In one battle, an ordinary Soviet soldier, Aleksandr

4

Koryavin, covered his commander, Lieutenant Ivonin, with his own body. Posthumously, Aleksandr was awarded the title Hero of the Soviet Union. But do you think at that moment he thought he was performing a heroic act? He simply was defending another man's life with his own body. Sometimes, too, one has to kill for the sake of saving another life. That is war. We didn't invent it, but having been in a war, we understand the meaning of the word. And all the more dear to us is that other word—peace. And what's the point if some seventeen-year-old kid calls you a killer and then goes out that night and beats up another like himself—three against one, even? That's why I don't believe words. Afghanistan taught me to believe actions, not words. There, guys were tested in action; everything was up front and clear. But not everyone was able to stand up to the test.

Some people consider all Afghantsi wonderful guys. From others you'll hear, "Afghantsi? Oh yeah, one of those types." Why do they want to lump us all together under one cliché? Afghantsi—it is not a profession, not even a calling; it's simply a name. Not everyone should, not everyone can, bear this name. We had a sergeant in our company who fulfilled his staff duties 100 percent and even more. For cleanliness and orderliness, our company was simply the best. But he never went to battle, our sergeant, and he never fired a shot, unlike all the others. And he went home with a *battle* medal. Why? I don't understand it myself.

Unfortunately, there were cowards there, and there were a few creeps there. And that's why the other kinds of guys, the ones I could go through fire and water with, that's why they are so dear to me: Oleg Loginov, Andrei Gaivoronski, Sergei Artemyev, Oleg Zaitsev, Sergei Matveyev, Sashka Tsvet. They are the real Afghantsi. But if you see a guy beating his breast and crowing, "Hey, I was in Afghanistan, I'm a vet. And you, here, what did you do?" that guy is not a real Afghanets. The war doesn't make a creep into a better person. He will come back the same as he left. So if you meet one of us, check him out first. Find out who and what he really is. After all, everyone is different. But if an Afghanets should turn to you for help, don't turn away from him, try to understand him. Unfortunately, not enough understanding is shown toward us. Many people think: Well, you came back from there, so, good for you. Rest a month or so, and come on, get back into the swing of things quickly. Get back to work, get moving! But war, after all, is not a film clip. You can't tear it out of your memory. The war will always live with us.

In the United States there are 186 psychological rehabilitation centers open to help Vietnam veterans. But where are we in the Soviet Union to go for help? We don't even have one such center. And so we look for that kind of help from people. That is when we run up against misunderstandings. From these misunderstandings comes the high divorce rate among Afghan vets, from these misunderstandings comes the turning inward, into oneself.

Not every person, after all, has the strength to beat his head against the wall of misunderstanding day after day: "What is the matter with him? What does he need, after all? What is he looking for?" It's at this point that another war starts, more bloody than *there*, and it cripples and maims a hundredfold more victims. And here the fight begins against yourself, on a battlefield without bullets. Is it better to defend your position, to stand up for yourself, or is it simply easier to stand off to one side?

For many, this inner battle takes the form of an angry protest against the unfamiliar: DOWN WITH PUNKS, ROCKERS, BREAK-DANCERS! But why? Better to try to understand a person than to protest against that which is strange and foreign to you. I myself did a lot of break-dancing when I came back from Afghanistan. I worked in a professional dance troupe. For me, break-dancing is a language without words, one which I can speak freely. A language of movement. But in order to speak that language, we had to work very hard. And many people were surprised: "You're an Afghanets, and you're break-dancing?"

One time our dance group met with the Yale University Slavic Chorus, which sings beautifully in Russian and English. We went to see them off at the Moscow railroad station. We started dancing for them, there on the platform, and they began to sing us Russian songs. It was unforgettable, the way the whole Moscow railroad station clapped wildly for us. But when they'd gotten on the train and gone, I saw one young guy who'd been watching them with a rage and fury so strong that I couldn't stop myself from going up to him. Then I heard him say: "I was in Afghanistan! And those shits! Their rockets..." I felt pain and sorrow for him. He was blaming the American people for the American rockets. The American people, who, I'm sure, like the majority of us, sincerely want peace and hate war.

Not long ago I took part in a meeting of Afghan vets and American Vietnam vets. Among them was one American who had lost both his legs in Vietnam, to Soviet rockets. And he had come to this meeting, to help Afghan vets maimed in the Afghan war by teaching them to make prosthetic devices. What else is there to say?

Often I am asked, "Did you get used to death, over there?"

No, I never got used to it. You can't get used to it. It's impossibly hard to believe in death, though you can feel its presence really close. I had a buddy from another company. Once, before a battle, he asked me to photograph him, to send a picture home to his wife. We had only twenty-four hours before the battle, but I rushed and was able to print his photograph. While I watched, he stuck it in an envelope and sealed it. When I returned, I learned he'd been killed. I couldn't believe it for a long time. It just seemed like he'd gone off somewhere, home maybe. And only when I came to his company and saw his neatly made cot, his beret and uniform on his pillow, then and only then did I realize he was dead. And the sharp sensation of the death of someone, someone who had been truly dear to you.

But I returned home. And I'm glad we are returning.

APPLICATION FOR TRAVEL ABROAD	
1. Last Name	TAMAROV
2. First Name, Patronymic	Vladislav Evgenievich
3. Date/Place of Birth	January 12, 1965 Leningrad
4. Nationality	Russian
5. Marital Status	Divorced
6. Party Affiliation	None
7. Profession	Free-lance photographer
8. Destination/ Purpose of Visit	USA Member of delegation of Soviet veterans of Afghanistan to visit American veterans of Vietnam.
9. Date of Application	April 24, 1989

Boot Camp

You could say that it all started in 1977. The Supreme Soviet was adopting a new Constitution for the nation. One of the articles said: "To serve in the Soviet army is the honorable duty of Soviet citizens." When they voted, everyone raised a hand, and the text of the Constitution was accepted unanimously. Not one person was against it; no one even vacillated. A new joyous holiday was added to our calendar: October 7, Constitution Day. But there was one more small item in the Constitution, Article 6. It addressed the role of the Communist party as director and supervisor of the USSR. So in 1979 four leaders of this same Communist party had a discussion and decided to send Soviet troops into Afghanistan. "In order to provide aid to the people of Afghanistan." No one asked us, the Soviet citizens, whether we wanted to fulfill *this* "honorable duty," whether we needed *this* "director and supervisor," whether we wanted to provide *this* "aid to the people of Afghanistan."

Yes. You could say that it started just like that.

I was awakened by a painfully recognizable and familiar sound. But in the barracks everyone else was sleeping. I stepped outside and sat down on the doorstep just outside the entrance. A light rain quietly crackled on the asphalt. I could hardly believe that I had been awakened by this barely audible sound. I wanted to forget about it and go home. Quietly, so as not to disturb my parents, I would open the door, and scurry into my room, and fall asleep to the crackling of Leningrad rain, which tapped against the window in tiny droplets. I would wake up in the morning, not to the cry of a sergeant ("Company! Reveille!"), but simply from the desire not to sleep anymore.

"Company! Reveille!" Before I could even wake up, my hands mechanically started to stuff my body into my rough army uniform. "Company! Outside for morning exercises!" I had to tie my shoelaces on the way out. The exercises started with a run, and that suited me fine. Before the army, I had run for distance. So on that score I had no problems—my sides didn't ache and it was no skin off my butt. But after the run came the most difficult part. Pull-ups. We had to do ten of them. I could do about eighteen, but that didn't matter. In the Soviet army, what matters is the collective effort. So after we had done ten pull-ups, we had to hang there like overripe apples until everyone else was done. We had to hang there a long time—they had hurried to collect anyone they could find for boot camp (since they knew where we were going from there)—and half of the recruits got stuck on the fourth or fifth pull-up.

Someone probably thought that group pull-ups was the way to strengthen the bonds among the members of our friendly collective. But the training only produced a herd mentality: the weak ones were defeated by the routine, and by the end of boot camp I could do only seven pull-ups. Many of the officers didn't care much about all that. Their assignment was to prepare cannon fodder to be sent to Afghanistan. They knew that during three or four months of boot camp they couldn't make us into anything much. Only a few of them tried to teach us at least something: hand-to-hand combat or marksmanship.

After breakfast, we usually had political lectures. For the first few days, we listened attentively, and were told how many American bases with how many nuclear missiles surrounded our defenseless Soviet Union; how important it was to protect the southern border of our motherland; how national self-defense required us to go to Afghanistan. (Who needs an international duty? Who wants to help the people of Afghanistan when decaying, rotting capitalism is trying to strangle the Soviet land that is ablossom with fully developed socialism!) At the beginning, we listened to all this in horror and let it seep into our eighteen-year-old hearts. But we knew all that stuff only too well: we had read about it in our newspapers; we had covered it in school; we had seen it on TV; we had heard it on the radio. So we soon reallocated the lecture period to a more useful purpose—we slept. What's more, we slept intelligently—sitting up, sometimes even with open eyes and with an attentive expression frozen on our faces.

But today I couldn't sleep. The rain, as before, tapped against the window in a way that reminded me of home. I had an unbearable desire to return home. For a person who loves his freedom, the stupid army rules were impossible to understand. To understand anything at all about the army was impossible. Even now I cannot find answers to some questions:

Why did they try to transform us into a colorless, anonymous herd that thought only about feeding its face and sleeping? A herd that was driven even to the toilet in formation.

Why did they feed us tasteless shit and pay us five rubles a month for personal expenses?

Why did they train us to jump with a parachute when they knew that no one used parachutes in Afghanistan?

Why was a soldier treated like an unthinking animal that had no rights other than to carry out stupid orders?

Why did the officers force us to believe things that they didn't believe themselves?

Why?

"I just want to get to Afghanistan, the sooner the better," I thought. "Everything will have to be different there . . ."

"Company! Reveille!" Before I could even wake up, my hands mechanically started to stuff my body into my rough Afghan uniform. The circle was closed and locked tight.

JULY 1984   FERGANA, SOVIET UNION   BOOT CAMP

Soldiers in the Soviet Airborne Forces are required to do a minimum of twelve parachute jumps, three every six months for two years. I was supposed to have six months' training in boot camp, but our officers were in a hurry—they knew we could be sent off earlier. More than half our time in boot camp was devoted to parachute training, and in my first three months there, I made the required three jumps. Two weeks after my last jump, I was flown to Afghanistan...

Where nobody made parachute jumps, which they'd trained me for.
Where I became a minesweeper, which I was never trained for.
Where I lived, to kill.
Where I killed, to live.

July 1984   Fergana, Soviet Union   Boot Camp

We were drafted at age eighteen. We had no choice. If you weren't in college, if you weren't disabled, if your parents didn't have a lot of money—then you were required to serve. Some young men broke their legs, some paid money; I enrolled in college. I didn't want to waste two years of my life, especially since I knew what awaited me in our army. But when I was in my second year of college, they changed the law, and took me. "Anywhere but Afghanistan," my mom said when she saw me off.

In boot camp, when I made my first jump, I was terrified to take the first step out of the plane . . . into the abyss.

When I took off for Afghanistan from boot camp, I was terrified to take the first step into the plane . . . into the abyss.

Combat Missions

People often ask me questions: How was it? What happened in Afghanistan? Why did the war start? What were we doing there, and how did we do it? And even, what kind of weapons did we use to do it? It's much easier for me to answer when I simply give people the information they want. In such conversations, I offer the dry numbers and use "official" words. And I try not to think about what lies behind them.

So, to begin at the beginning.

The Afghan government came to power in April 1978 after a military coup. This new government repeatedly asked the Soviet Union for help in supporting its regime. In response, Soviet troops entered Afghanistan in December 1979. This decision was made by four members of the Politburo of the Communist party of the Soviet Union, and became known publicly only after the deaths of all four, through official announcements in the Soviet press. If another member of our government dies of old age, it could possibly turn out that he took part in the decision too. But in this story, it's not important.

The first (and official) reason for sending Soviet troops into Afghanistan was to satisfy the request of the Afghan government.

A second reason: Afghanistan is the Soviet Union's southern neighbor, and placing troops there assured the relative security of our southern borders. The Soviet press didn't write about this reason, but new recruits were told during basic training in boot camp that it was precisely for this reason that they were going to Afghanistan.

Recently, reports are starting to seep out about a third reason, although the information mysteriously keeps disappearing. During the war, there was a constant traffic in drugs, gold, and precious stones from Afghanistan into the Soviet Union. There were cases in which zinc coffins were sent to the USSR filled with narcotics instead of soldiers' bodies. To this day, such incidents are covered up, as is the trail of money from this business. Probably, the trail leads too high. But in this story, again, it's not important.

The 40th Army and the 103d Airborne Division were sent to Afghanistan. Border guards took part in some combat missions, operating from the territory of the Soviet Union, but the primary military burden fell on the 103d Airborne Division, which had four regiments in Afghanistan. One regiment, the commanding officers, and the Special Division Battalions were located around the Kabul airfield. A second regiment was stationed near the Afghan government residence in Kabul; one of its duties was to protect the residence. The third, my regiment, was headquartered at the Bala-Hisar fortress on the outskirts of Kabul. A fourth regiment was stationed at the Bagram airport, not far from the capital.

Airborne troops (*decantniki*) are considered the elite of the Soviet army. They receive the best preparation and special training because they have a specific mission: to be dropped at a moment's notice anywhere on the planet to carry out military operations without support troops. So every airborne regiment has its own medics, radiomen, minesweepers, artillery, tanks, and so on. And unlike other units, airborne troops take orders only from the airborne high command and the Soviet defense minister himself.

Before being sent to Afghanistan, airborne units were supposed to complete a special six-month training course in the Soviet Union. For other kinds of troops, training was just a formality and lasted only a few weeks, except for the special troops, the landing storm troops. These units received the same training (and even wore the same uniform) as the airbornes, but their mission was to land inside enemy territory, up to ninety miles from the front lines, and act in the interests of the army to which they were attached.

The mountainous terrain of Afghanistan defined our basic (if not our only) strategy: to always be higher than the enemy. During combat missions special groups were sent ahead, or dropped in advance by helicopters, onto the highest points to cover for the main troops.

Soviet troops carried out four types of military actions in Afghanistan:

1. Major operations were carried out by the 103d Division, with support from the special troops of the 40th Army, using artillery and aircraft. The Afghan government army also participated. The goal of such operations was to destroy large groups of Mujahadeen in specific regions of Afghanistan. Such operations were carried out in stages, and went on for several weeks or sometimes longer.

2. Small operations were usually carried out by one regiment; artillery and aircraft were also used. The goal of these smaller operations was to target and destroy a specific group of Mujahadeen, whose location had been discovered by Afghan intelligence. These missions rarely lasted longer than ten days.

3. "Combing" villages often went on concurrently with the combat missions. The goal was to find hidden weapons or Mujahadeen hospitals.

4. Ambushes were carried out by small groups, usually by a company of scouts, and were organized near the roads, on mountain trails, and near villages. Usually the ambushes were planned from information obtained by Afghan intelligence. But some ambushes were staged as preventive measures, on the roads most frequently used by the Mujahadeen.

Troops were transported to the site of military operations by helicopters or by military convoys.

Combat missions were carried out frequently in the summertime; they became less frequent as winter approached. When it was cold, the Mujahadeen tried to get back to Pakistan, or they came down from the mountains into the villages. Even in the winter, they sometimes attacked Soviet convoys carrying ammunition, weapons, and food from the Soviet Union.

Near the big cities and busy roads, permanent encampments were set up, where fifteen to forty Soviet soldiers lived. They also guided artillery fire.

Their task was to control the area and guard the roads. In case of emergency, they would call for help by radio.

Besides ordinary artillery, Soviet troops in Afghanistan used two kinds of rocket launchers: GRAD (Russian for "hail") and URAGAN (Russian for "hurricane"). Aircraft included the jet-propelled MIG and SU and the AN airplane. MI-8 helicopters were used for transport: carrying troops, ammunition, water, and food. MI-24 helicopters, quick and accurate in fire power, were used to cover troops and the MI-8s; they were almost never used for transport.

The Mujahadeen didn't have aircraft or heavy artillery. Their "heaviest" weapons were rocket launchers for ground-to-ground and ground-to-air Stingers, recoilless light mountain cannons, mortars, and large-caliber machine guns—DShKs.

Soviet troops also used DShKs, as well as PTRC guided missile launchers, unguided NURS missiles, "vacuum" missiles called SHMELs (Russian for "bumblebee"), and mortars. Our soldiers carried Kalashnikov automatics. In the 40th Army, the model was an AK-47 (7.62 mm caliber), while the airborne and the landing storm troops had AKS-74s (5.45 mm caliber). The latter weapon's smaller-caliber bullet caused greater bodily injury. Also, the AKS-74 had a metal, not a wooden, folding rifle butt, which made it more compact to carry when you made a parachute landing. Drivers and pilots often used the AKSU, a short-barreled model of the AKS-74.

Both sides used many other kinds of weapons in Afghanistan, but I don't have the heart to talk about that anymore.

For the USSR, the war ended on February 15, 1989, when the pullout of Soviet troops was completed.

For the 15,000(?) Soviet soldiers and the approximately 1,000,000 Afghans who perished, the war had ended much earlier.

This is a page from my Afghan notebook. Here, I wrote down each of my combat missions. First, I wrote down the mission number. If I'd been in the mountains, I circled the number. Then I wrote the name of the place where we'd been and how many days we were there. Last, I wrote the month and the year. That was my system.

Once, back home, I decided to count how many days out of my twenty months in Afghanistan I'd been on combat missions: 217 days. And I'm still paying the price for every one of those days.

"Let them be quick," he said quietly, staring fixedly at the sky. Blood had seeped through the bandages on his chest, and I had to change them. I took out a new bandage, but he stopped me with his hand: "Do you hear? It's the copters!"

I listened intently . . . he was right. A few minutes later, the helicopters were circling above us, looking for a landing site.

"Don't be scared; you'll make it," I tried to encourage him. But he didn't hear me—he'd lost consciousness again.

We found this cache of weapons a few hours before this picture was taken. We'd never have found it by ourselves; it was buried too deep in the ground. An Afghan defector from the Mujahadeen pointed it out to us, and all we had to do was dig it up and load it in the helicopters. One of our officers was even decorated for unearthing this cache.

But when I look at these two pictures, I think about something else. There were several land-to-land missiles in this cache, and I'd once seen the launching of such a missile. It happened a year earlier, a few kilometers from this site. It was the third time that I'd been on a combat mission in my first two months, and when I heard the lieutenant's command, "Rest!" I joyfully threw myself down in the shade of a big rock that was overhanging the path. We'd been climbing this mountain for three hours, but we could still see our support convoy, which had set up temporary camp in the valley below. I heard a strange noise behind me. Someone was swearing loudly. Looking out from under the rock, I saw a quick flash on the next slope, about a mile away. And immediately following—a bright yellow arrow whizzed at incredible speed in the camp's direction.

"What's that?" I asked Sergei Artemyev. He didn't hear me.

"Camp! Camp! Do you read me?! There's a rocket coming at you!" the radioman shouted openly into his receiver, abandoning codes. But then he stopped. A flash glittered in the camp, raising a small cloud of dust. From where we sat, it was a strange spectacle: tiny figures bustling about in total silence around the place where the rocket had hit. We were all quiet, as if awaiting something. The radio crackled, trying to make contact with us.

"How many?" Sergei asked the radioman.

"Three," he replied, turning away.

"Forward!" the lieutenant quietly ordered, pulling the bolt on his automatic.

It was a lot easier on us when the helicopters took us into the mountains: you went to the airfield, boarded the copter, and in an hour you were there. And there—well, you're on your own. When we went by convoy, there were always lots of problems: checking the road, and the dust and wind. The trip was always long and uncomfortable, and they unloaded us far from where we were supposed to end up. Sometimes we had to spend a couple of days climbing mountains just to get into the right quadrant. Getting back to the base by convoy was even worse.

We descended to the road very late at night. We'd spent many hours searching for the body of one of our guys, until the Mujahadeen realized why we still hadn't left. Then, in the darkness, they brought his body closer to us. I was dead tired, but the convoy had been waiting for us for more than a day. We'd been due to come back as soon as possible; the next day we were to be dropped off at another site.

While I was deciding which armored personnel carrier to get on, the convoy started to move. One of the guys reached for me, and I jumped on to the closest one. I got the place nearest to the turret, in front. On one hand, it was always colder there because of the wind, and the dust that blew into your face wasn't so great either. But on the other hand, you could hang on to the barrel of the turret, which I did . . . When I woke up, it was morning. My numb arm still clung to the barrel, and it was hard to unclench it. We were already approaching Kabul.

Zhenye Parukov, who'd been my partner on this mission, turned out to be sitting next to me. "The convoy was fired on last night," he informed me.

"Did they get me?" I started to joke, but stumbled on my words: there was one guy missing from our carrier.

Ambush. A short, sharp word. Usually we found out we were going on one unexpectedly, but simply: "This evening, the scout company is going on an ambush. They need two minesweepers."

. . . We'd been going for several hours. A bright white moon lit up the valley with merciless light; we kept having to hide in the long shadows cast by the mountains. And the longer we walked, the higher the moon rose, the shorter the shadows became. In an hour, we'd have no place left to hide. In that cold light, we were easy targets. I never knew that night could be brighter than day. I wanted to fall down, hide, and wait for the sun to rise.

This turned out to be a quiet day for us. From above, we were covering our guys who were "working" below. On this day, I even managed to get enough sleep. Late in the evening, they climbed back up to where we were. Walking past them, I tripped; someone was sleeping right on the path. I wanted to swear, but before I could—the wind whipped back the covering, and I saw their identical white, angular faces.

33

When I came home, I was asked to put my pictures in a photo exhibit at the Cinematography College, where I'd enrolled upon returning. This picture—me standing with an arm around an Afghan government soldier—was one of three photos I gave them for the exhibit. For the exhibit, I gave this photo a short, bogus title: They Defend the Revolution.

My pictures won first prize, and when they gave me this "honestly earned" award, I began to ask myself what I was doing, and why.

A few months after the exhibit, I dropped out of college, left my wife, and began to write this book.

Mujahadeen prisoners of war. We didn't keep them chained together, and we didn't torture them in prisons. We turned them over·to the Afghan government troops. And what did they do with them? If they were caught without any weapons, they were shaved and recruited into the government army. I remember a time when we met seven shepherds herding sheep in the mountains. They had no weapons on them, and we didn't have the right to touch them. Even though there were seven shepherds for only fifteen sheep.

These are prisoners. A few hours ago, they were free men in the mountains, but now they are here in our camp. Now they are silently looking us over, while we are silently looking them over. But it wasn't always like this...

He was holding his right leg, but the blood soaked through his fingers and flowed over his hand onto his sleeve. Intuition had served me again this time: my kick had knocked his automatic out of his grasp a fraction of a second before he could press the trigger. The second kick was to his face. It sent him flying about six feet. I set my sights on his head, but something stopped me. "He is only a boy?!" I observed and lowered my automatic. At the same moment, one of our guys let out a yelp behind me. Another bullet whistled by right next to me. Apparently, this Mujahadeen was not the only one here. Again I aimed at his head, but again something stopped me. I saw how his hands were trembling; I noticed the horror in his eyes. "He is only a boy!" I thought and pressed the trigger.

The column was built by the troops of Alexander the Great many centuries ago. By the same Alexander the Great who said, "One can occupy Afghanistan, but one cannot vanquish her." This column, visible from Kabul, stood in this same place when Alexander the Great and his troops left Afghanistan; it stood there when our troops came into Afghanistan, and it remained standing even after our troops left Afghanistan.

I never ever sat like this, in such an open and vulnerable position. I just liked the view from this cliff, and I decided to take this shot especially for my parents: to show how peaceful it was in Afghanistan.

I set up the shot, gave the camera to my friend, and sat down on the rock. But within two seconds, I wasn't *anywhere* near that rock.

Panjsher

Panjsher—its name means "Valley of Five Lions."

Panjsher—one of the most dangerous places in Afghanistan.

Panjsher—one of the most beautiful places I've ever seen.

Panjsher—I was there three times, but three times I came back.

The explosion rang in my ears with an unexpectedly sharp force. Out of habit, my body reacted to it faster than my mind—in an instant, I was already lying in the bushes. I could hear nothing but the sound of my own heartbeat. Directly in front of me, a frightened ant rocked back and forth on a blade of grass in a state of indecision, as if he were deciding whether he should run back or continue along a path that only he knew. After lying there a few more seconds, just in case, I finally got up. I casually brushed myself off and, for some reason, with a guilty smile I motioned to an old lady with my index finger at my temple to show that I was crazy. "This is too much," I thought as I walked by a truck driver who was kicking his flat tire in disappointment.

. . . "Mama has come home," I guessed, when I heard the click of the lock in the corridor. There was no place to hide the vodka. And besides, it was already too late. As she entered the kitchen she just threw up her hands in despair: "Are you drinking again? You've been back a month! Maybe you've had enough?!" It was going to take her a while, so all I could do was finish what was in my glass and go to my room. I felt sorry for her, but even I didn't understand what was happening to me. . .

. . . The explosion rang in my ears with an unexpectedly sharp force. Out of habit, my body reacted to it faster than my mind—in an instant, I was already lying behind a big rock, against a cliff a few feet from the trail. There was no blood. That meant everyone was alive. Thank God for that. They were shooting from somewhere above us. We had passed through there about twenty minutes ago. OK, so the *Dushmans* ("the bandits," as we called the Mujahadeen) had decided to begin launching mines, and it was a strange sort of favor for them to do for us—because had they started with the large-caliber machine gun, the DShK, there would have been nothing left of us but holes when they finished.

Under the rock, something started to rustle—a young scorpion, with his tail in the air, like a tomcat on the prowl, froze in his attack stance. Clearly, this place wasn't big enough for both of us. Since, after all, I was older, I had to throw him out onto the trail. He was obviously dissatisfied with his new location and he ran off in short bursts of speed to another rock, about thirty feet behind me. This was not the scorpion's lucky day, however. Behind the rock, someone cursed a blue streak and shot him with a round of fire from an automatic. "It's a good thing he didn't use his grenades, too," I thought. I recognized the voice of the artillery gun-layer. He wasn't a bad guy, but he was high-strung. In any event, there were now two of us to get out of there. The one in front covers. He attracts the fire while the one in back runs. The situation isn't particularly pleasant for either person. In this case, the artillery gun-layer was behind me.

Drops of salty sweat slowly crawled down my unshaven cheek and stuck in the corner of my mouth. I really didn't want to die, and nobody was asking me to. After arguing a while over whether he should run on a count of three or five, we agreed on seven. There was a smell of lemon in the air. There was no way to tell where it was coming from. I wanted to wake up, and the sooner the better.

. . . On Sundays, I usually slept in, until Mama let the hungry cat into my room. Koozia was orange but fat and always hungry. My parents had bought me the kitten when I was in the seventh grade. Then he was so tiny that I could close my fingers around him in the palm of my hand. Now, when he comes to me at night to get warm, he takes up the better half of the bed. He usually jumps up on the bed, sticks his wet nose in my ear, and purrs into it.

As usual, the tickling wakes me up this morning. I put on my robe and slippers, take the cat under my arm, and walk into the kitchen. My father, as always, is shaving at the table, while Mama sets my morning tea in front of me . . . with lemon.

. . . A mine crackled close by and exploded about fifteen feet from the artillery gun-layer. We needed to get our asses out of there as fast as we could. There was no time to lose, so I threw four smoke bombs onto the trail, all that I had. The artillery gun-layer started to count. The pungent red smoke spread out like a half-transparent cloud over the incline, and I could feel my fury pinning down my body tighter and tighter. I couldn't die, Mom and Dad were waiting for me at home. They were forty-six years old, and they had devoted twenty of those years to me. Now I wasn't thinking about myself; I was thinking of them. On the count of seven, my finger pressed the trigger, which was shiny with use. In my heart there was nothing but frenzy and fury; I was ready to destroy every living thing around me, whether it was human or not. A bullet buzzed right by my ear and slapped into the cliff behind my back. "Exploders," I noticed mechanically, while my hand replaced one magazine after another. The next incoming bullet knocked off my hat. THAT'S IT! I was already pressing my back into the cliff and trying to get my finger, which was numb with tension, off the trigger.

. . . The door opened. It was Mama. I barely recognized her—she sat for a while with horrible bags under her eyes. Tears fell right onto her wrinkled, trembling hands. Dad was crying somewhere in the kitchen. How she had aged over these two years.

. . . Bullets slapped into the cliff a few inches from me. The fragments fell under my legs and rolled toward the trail. It's better that they're exploders—at least they won't hit me when they ricochet off the rock. OK, now I'm the target and it won't be so easy to get out of here. It was getting pretty noisy—the Mujahadeen obviously didn't expect this kind of impudence from us, and now they were shooting with whatever was at hand. A shell crackled through the air and exploded somewhere up around where they were shooting from. Then a second, a third. That was a pleasant change—it meant that the artillery gun-layer had made it and now he was directing the artillery fire. He was covering me. "It's a good thing he didn't call out the air force, too," I thought, but I had to get myself together and I still had to resolve a final question: to run with my backpack or without it. On one hand, in my backpack were the mine-finder, my camera, and two rolls of film I had shot. On the other hand, I had a lot of useful, but heavy, trash in there.

I put the pack on, took it off again, but then decided to run with it. (I couldn't stand losing the camera and the film.) And still the question, Where is that lemon smell coming from? Now came the most difficult part—like jumping with a parachute—the first step, a step off a precipice. And it was a long way to run, about 105 feet. But if I really tried, I could make it in about ten seconds. I wasn't scared, but for some reason I was stuck to the cliff. The next shell crackled in the air. The Mujahadeen froze. Explosion! Now! Let's go . . .

ONE! My body went soft after the first step . . .

TWO! No thoughts of any kind. There was no place to fall. Eyes—forward . . .

THREE! Forward . . . Forward . . .

FOUR! Why the hell did I bring this backpack?

FIVE! Damn this Panjsher!!!

SIX! Relax. The guys are already covering me.

SEVEN! Where is the ground?! I fell into emptiness . . .

EIGHT! A bullet whistled somewhere behind me. If I hadn't fallen, it would have hit me in the head . . .

NINE! The ground hit me in the back with frightening force. Something blindingly blue cut across my eyes . . .

. . . At one time I was little. But even then, things were complicated between my parents and me. I was always getting into trouble. Once, when I was about six, a boy from next door picked a fight with me. That made me so mad that I picked up a stick off the ground and walked right up to him. He was obviously scared to death. He grabbed a rock and started to yell so that I would stop coming toward him. But I kept coming, and I wasn't the least bit afraid. He was the one who was scared... A rock grazed my temple. Something unpleasant and sticky rolled down my cheek and I fell down for some reason. Right before my eyes a blindingly blue sky beckoned me toward it. I wanted to stretch myself far enough to touch it. Somebody's hands lifted me up. Mama! She was running somewhere and crying as she went, while I kept trying to get away and give him what for...

TEN!... It's the sky. But why is it so bright?

ELEVEN!... It's so close that I can reach out and stroke it...

TWELVE!... Somebody's hands grabbed me and dragged me behind the rocks.

THIRTEEN!... I seem to be coming to. Somebody is taking off my backpack.

FOURTEEN! Why the hell am I counting?! Enough! I made it!

I looked up to where the steep descent began. Alas, I hadn't noticed it... but I flew pretty well, about twelve feet. "What are you lying around for?" smiled the tired artillery gun-layer. "This is Panjsher. It's not a place for relaxing," he said. He was right, Panjsher is definitely not a place for relaxing. I had learned that lesson again in autumn, when I was there a second time. That day we were already headed back to the base, and our minesweepers' armored transport went, as always, at the front of our convoy.

...The road had already evened out. We had passed the dangerous part and we could relax. I knew that the convoy was behind us, although it was impossible to make out anything behind the clouds of dust raised by our armored car. I leaned back on my backpack. Bright white clouds were moving behind the distant mountains. They were surrounded by a thin veil of morning smoke, as they descended—one jagged ledge after the next—toward the road below. It was impossible to tell whether they were far away or very close. A frightened little hedgehog scurried away from the thundering road full of iron vehicles.

Still, it was so damned beautiful. I was digging through my backpack, looking for my camera... Something big and strong struck from below. The air was filled with some kind of strange, gooey silence—as if you could swim in it. My hands stretched out in front of me, while I looked down at myself from somewhere up above and saw my body tearing itself off the armored transport in pursuit of my hands. I was swimming up somewhere into this gooey silence. It seemed that if this silence had been any thicker, I would have gotten stuck in it... forever. But my body started to turn over in the air slowly, even lazily, and floated to the ground. The burrs punctured my hands. "Shit! I got a sliver," I thought in despair.

At that moment, the silence was torn apart by a deafening roar. Our armored transport was speeding right over the rocks away from the road. "Just like that hedgehog," I smiled. I pulled myself together—we probably hit a rock, and I fell off like a greenhorn. The guys will start laughing now. Then I saw whose mug, yellow with dust, was laughing at me from the other side of the road. So they were laughing at me, I guessed. Only after I looked at him long and hard did I recognize Oleshka Loginov. His appearance was rather amusing, his whole face filthy with dust and some kind of soot. Only a bright red line starting right under his nose and dripping in red-brown drops from his chin distinguished itself on his face. Hey, why is he laughing? You ought to see yourself! The sickeningly sweet smell of blood hit my nose. "That's all I needed," I thought and started mechanically to rub it off my chin.

Somebody was yelling. When I lifted my head, I saw the platoon commander running toward us from the armored transport. Why is he causing a panic? Doesn't he see that everybody is alive and healthy? But then I noticed that Oleshka Loginov was pointing at something with his finger. A deep mine-crater had torn the road apart and all around it were black fragments of the armored transport tires. "We blew up!" I understood. The platoon commander ran up: "You alive?! Well, OK. Let's go. We need to check the road ahead."

. . . No, Panjsher is not a place for relaxing. I looked around: the artillery gun-layer was staring at my twisted mine-detector, and right behind him a "pill" (as we called the medics) was pulling a grenade splinter out of somebody's ass. It was an amusing sight. I would have even laughed, but not here, not now. I heard the voice of Miroshnechenko. I knew him from basic training. He was a reliable guy. With a guy like that, you can go behind enemy lines. In fact, I had already gone behind the lines with him.

Here in Afghanistan Miroshnechenko had become a radio operator. He even had his own room where they stored the walkie-talkies, and I often went to his room to print pictures when we came back from battle. But now, he was in a less-than-desirable situation. A sniper had "found" him, and it wasn't going to be easy for him to get to us. The worst of it was that we couldn't help him— he was too far away. "Comrade, ensign! Run! I will cover you!" he yelled. That's funny, where did he find an ensign? But when I looked harder, I noticed a curled-up figure in the rocks. Aha! There he is. But it seems that the ensign had expressed no particular desire to run first and motioned for Miroshnechenko to go ahead. "Then cover me," yelled Miroshnechenko and ran toward us. The ensign raised his automatic from behind the rock and started to "cover" him. The bullets bounced off the rocks about fifteen feet from him and ricocheted off to the side. You shit! My fury shook my whole body in a seizure; so many good guys were killed because of that kind of worm. My hand took the automatic off my shoulder and cocked it. In the mountains, the rules are different. It's not important whether you're a colonel or a soldier. Everything is decided by those who can decide and are worthy of deciding. But if you're a coward and others can be killed because of you—who will ever figure out from whose bullet you croaked?

My finger cold-bloodedly moved for the trigger—but somebody's hand knocked the gun out of my grasp, and the round went off high in the sky. "He has children at home!" rasped the artillery gun-layer, but I saw that he was shaking no less than I was.

Somebody was waiting at home for each of us. Parents, friends, wives, children. But why did the best among us so often turn out to be the ones who were killed, while the bastards kept coming back? They returned home in order to pound on their chest and yell that I, the shit, spilled blood in Afghanistan. Only the blood was not his own, but somebody else's. The blood of those who came here for nothing and were killed for no one. The blood of those who came here as children and returned as old men. Who will answer for this blood?

The helicopter had just let us out here. We didn't know exactly where we were; we didn't even know why we were here. We fired at everything that fired at us. But over the radio someone told us where we were supposed to go. We didn't know why we should go there, and therefore we went. All night we climbed to the very top; once we got there, we got the order to go back down immediately. We asked them where we were going, but they answered that our job was not to ask questions, but to follow orders. And we went. And we came to a place that we didn't know for a reason that we didn't understand. There was something insane about all of this—as if no one knew what we were doing here.

The day began quietly. We were firing occasional shots, covering the scout pla-toon that was climbing the mountain. Periodically, their radioman would call us and report, "Everything's OK. We're making it up the mountain. No prob-lems, it's just real hot."

It *was* real hot; I even dozed off, warming myself in the sun . . .

"We have two twenty-ones!" The terrified cry of the radioman jolted me awake. Within a few seconds, we were rushing to help them. Two twenty-ones meant two dead; that meant they'd been ambushed; that meant . . .

"One twenty-one has come alive!" This time the radioman's voice was bewildered. We didn't climb the mountain; we raced up it—there was no time. We had lost our second wind about seven hundred yards back, and now we were on our sixth or seventh wind. From the direction where the scout platoon had gone, we heard the heavy double echoes of the Bur, an English sniper's rifle. Our guys were in deep shit.

"Where are you? They are *everywhere* here! We need help! Where the fuck are you?!" Throwing off our packs and leaving them behind with those who couldn't run anymore, we ran higher and higher. On the way, the artillery gun-layer called by radio for artillery help. "Where are you? Where the *fuck* are you?!" shouted the radioman, as we ran past him. With one hand he was squeezing his leg, but a thin dark-red stream trickled out from under his fingers and dripped quickly onto the dusty stones. The sugary smell of the blood made me want to fall down and shut my eyes. "Go on!"—he spotted me and waved his arm,—"the guys behind will get me!"

With my back, I felt something terrible coming. My body jumped behind a big rock; Miroshnechenko fell on top of me. It felt like I was lying on top of somebody as well. The shell exploded about seven yards from us. Thank God, it was *our* fire—they were just a little off.

We didn't know what would happen tomorrow. And we tried to forget what had happened yesterday.

We stayed here for only a few hours. We rested and went on. But the camera snatched this fraction of a second from the eternal flow of time and froze it forever. At this moment we didn't yet know that in a few hours we would fall into an ambush. At this moment, while we were filling our canteens from the stream, we didn't yet know that we would stay in the mountains for three days without a drop of water. We didn't yet know anything...

We didn't believe in tomorrow. And we couldn't forget what had happened yesterday.

Panjsher—I was there three times, but three times I came back.

At the moment this picture was taken, these scouts were being fired on. They had only ten or fifteen seconds to jump from the helicopter, take up good positions, and stay alive while doing so. Their job was to secure the landing area, so that the rest of the troops could land safely.

We could always tell the relative danger of a combat landing by how many troops were in each helicopter. If there were ten to twelve soldiers, then it wasn't a dangerous landing because we could take up to ten or fifteen seconds to get out. If there were eight soldiers that meant it was dangerous; we had even less time to get in the clear. If there were six of us, that meant it was very dangerous; we had only six seconds. This landing time had to be kept as short as possible because the helicopters were most vulnerable when they were on the ground. When we were in the air, it wasn't so terrifying because we knew that, even if we were hit, we could land by gliding, as long as the propellers hadn't been damaged.

This is why, when I'd served my time and was being flown home, I was really agitated. Because I knew that any stupid bullet could get our plane, and *this* plane couldn't glide to a safe landing. To this day, I'm scared to fly and every time I do, I carry sleeping pills with me. And I try not to sleep at all the night before a flight because the sleeping pills are often useless when I fly. Why? Because I know that this plane won't be able to glide to a safe landing either.

July 1985 Panjsher, Afghanistan

This Afghan was killed a few minutes ago. He was killed by a nineteen-year-old boy, by one of us. He was probably one of those who were shooting at us . . . but maybe not. It's possible that he was simply returning home . . . maybe not. In the mountains, we didn't have time to think, Is this a friend or an enemy? We only had time to pull the trigger . . . but maybe not. We shot at every shadow; everything that moved was a threat to us. In this strange game, he who killed first, won. And as a prize, he won the chance to play again. And we had no choice. And that's why we were right . . . but maybe not.

They sent us here when we were all of eighteen. But before that, they asked us, Do you want this or not? And we answered yes because we knew that if we answered no, we would end up here all the same. End up here so that more and more of these bodies would be left on this land.

JULY 1985   PANJSHER, AFGHANISTAN

Here I am again. In my hands is an anti-transport mine, a TS-6.1, made in Italy, which is how it got its nickname, the "Italian." I didn't disarm this mine on the road for one simple reason—it wasn't on the road. We had stopped here for a rest, and one of the guys noticed its jagged yellow side among the rocks. None of us knew what an anti-transport mine was doing in the rocks, far away from any roads, but in this case it didn't matter. It took me twenty minutes and about six pounds of sweat, but I managed to get it out of there. Under it, there was a second one. We didn't want to bring the mines with us—each one weighed about fifteen pounds—so we had to find something to blow up. Luckily, we didn't have to look for long. We went to get water from a small stream and found big sacks of flour hidden nearby. No one knew what the sacks were doing there but, under the circumstances, that also didn't matter. A few minutes later, both the mines and the flour sacks were flying skyward together toward God. Why did I do it? I don't know. Maybe that flour was being stored away for the winter. But for us, at that moment, it didn't matter. We were in an alien land. And why were we there? To this day, for some, it doesn't matter.

July 1985 Panjsher, Afghanistan

Yup, Panjsher is a truly beautiful place. Sometimes during quiet moments, I even forgot that there was a war. But that never lasted too long—Panjsher was not a place for relaxing.

It was near this stream that we found the hidden sacks of flour; so this is the last shot of this scenery—within a few minutes there'll be nothing left of this place but a deep black crater. And we'll go on, not thinking about what we left behind. We weren't cruel: that flour could have been meant for the enemy. And we didn't have time to think about what we left behind. We tried to believe that we were going forward, and we knew there was no going back.

The first few times I printed this picture, I tried to print it so that the faces were visible. But once I forgot to do it like that, and the people came out very dark. I put away that picture, thinking it was a lousy print, and forgot it.

A year later, I accidentally found it. And then it struck me how unnatural those dark figures were among the wheatfields and against the beautiful mountains. Why did it take almost two years after I came home for this thought to occur to me?

Those first two years after Afghanistan, I couldn't think seriously or deeply about anything. During those first two years I managed to marry, divorce, start college, drop out of college, and work as a laborer, a performer, and a streetsweeper. I couldn't understand why I couldn't stick with anything or anyone.

The first three or four months I was home, I couldn't even guess that I was in a fog. I understood this only when the fog suddenly lifted. I remember the moment it happened as if it were yesterday. I was riding home on the 107 bus, sitting by the window; a bright sun was shining.

Suddenly I see that the grass, as it turns out, is green; that means it's summer. And I see I'm on a bus, going where? I'm going home, to my home. I am home.

MINESWEEPERS

I knew right away that it would be a short conversation. Bright red clouds sped crazily across the sky, leaving vague traces dripping a bloody stream down into the valley. There wasn't much time left.

I tried to understand, was it morning or evening?—when suddenly I felt that *they* were nearby. This time, they were coming from behind. I couldn't see them, but I sensed with my back that they were getting closer.

"Hi," he said, almost whispering, and I turned around. Today there were only two of them: Sergei and Sasha. "This will be a short conversation," stressed Sergei, and sat down right on the rocks.

The last time, they had come to my home, but now we were somewhere in the mountains. It was uncomfortable here: the red sky was painfully blinding me, and it was hard to see them. Sasha sat next to Sergei, but I understood that today he would remain silent.

"We came to help," Sergei began.

"Help with what?" I didn't understand.

"Why do you need it?" He answered a question with a question.

"I don't know..." I was about to speak, but instead clammed up; I knew I was lying.

"So don't lie!" he reproached me, and looked unexpectedly straight into my eyes. My body trembled as an unpleasant cold ran through me.

"Who needs it?" he asked again.

I kept quiet; I didn't know the answer... The silence crushed me. He was waiting.

"I do." For some reason I could only whisper.

"What for?" he asked again, ruthlessly.

There was no getting away. I wanted to cover my ears and not hear his questions. I wanted to tell him that this was crazy, that I didn't have to answer

him. But I was scared of hurting his feelings. What if he doesn't know that he is dead?

I looked straight into his eyes: "I need it. So I can live for what is, not what was. I can't speak about this, but I can write it. I have to leave it behind me forever..."

"So, that's it," Sasha said thoughtfully.

"Yes, I guess so. Time to go," said Sergei. He stood up, stood up and began to walk away. I tried to stop him, but the faster I ran after them, the farther away they were. I ran faster and faster, but they grew farther and farther away. I was so tired I fell, and when I came to... soft morning light burst in through the curtains and a multicolored ray of light shone in the mirror. Small slippery drops of cold sweat dripped down my cheek and fell on the wrinkled sheet. She wasn't beside me; from the kitchen came the sound of running water. She's making breakfast. I understood: time to get up.

Unthinkingly, I pulled on my robe, stuck my feet inside my slippers, and started for the bathroom. I could smell an omelet cooking—it must be Sunday.

"Good morning!" she smiled.

"Uh huh," I answered and shut the door behind me. There was no cold water, again, so I had to brush my teeth with hot.

"They've shut off the cold water until Tuesday!" she shouted.

"Uh huh," I thought and stepped into the shower. But after a few unsuccessful attempts with the faucet, it got through to me that there was no cold water.

"Everything's ready," she called from the kitchen, and I went in to have breakfast.

"Happy holiday!" she smiled again and smacked me on the nose.

"What holiday?" I didn't understand.

"Your holiday," she answered uncertainly, and turned on the TV. While it was warming up, I glanced at the calendar and saw that it was May 9. Victory Day. War Victory Day. Not *my* war, but *ours*: the Great Patriotic War. The TV warmed up—a war movie was on. Not about my war, the one they tried to forget, but about our war, World War II, the war we won. The film was boring, but I watched the screen and mechanically drank my lukewarm coffee. I was reminded of my grandpa, who'd died a few years ago from a piece of shrapnel that had been stuck somewhere in his chest since that war. When I was a little kid, I never understood why he didn't like me watching war movies...

Unexpectedly, something painfully familiar flickered across the screen, bringing me back to reality. On the screen, minesweepers were checking a road. A sergeant was teaching a "green" soldier: "A minesweeper makes only two mistakes: the first is when he decides to be a minesweeper. The second—"

I don't know why, but I turned off the TV and locked myself in the bathroom. She banged on the door, shouting something at me, but I turned the water on full force so I couldn't hear her anymore.

The first when he decides to be one? We didn't have a chance to make this mistake: they ordered us to become minesweepers and we became minesweepers... I tried to understand, was it morning or evening?—when I suddenly felt that *they* were nearby. I wanted to tell them to go away, that they were dead, but I was scared to hurt their feelings. What if they didn't know? Didn't they know that they'd already made this mistake, back in 1985? When both of them were blown up on one mine. It was said that nothing much was left of them...

Someone once said that a minesweeper makes only two mistakes: the first is when he decides to be one. The second... An insistent pounding on the door brought me back. Time to go finish breakfast; it was getting cold.

In Afghanistan, one of the most respected professions among the soldiers was that of minesweeper. Without minesweepers along, no group ever went into the mountains, no car ever drove off the base, and no transport column ever set out along the road. There were mines everywhere: along the roads, on mountain paths, in abandoned houses. There were different kinds of mines: anti-transport and anti-personnel; mines that jumped out of the ground and mines that were activated by the vibrations of human steps; mines that killed any living thing for a radius of fifty meters; mines that were set off by radio and mines that were set off by mine-detectors. Often, bombs were placed under the mines, so that the explosions would be more powerful.

It was precisely on such a mine, one with a bomb underneath, that three minesweepers from my platoon were killed instantly in July 1985. Two others were gravely wounded, with severe concussions.

The names of those three minesweepers were not the last names to go on the list of those who had died in our platoon.

There were no safe roads in Afghanistan. That's why the mine trawler (a tank without a turret) or an armed personnel carrier with minesweepers aboard was first in the convoy. On dangerous parts of the road, where there might be mines, we stopped the convoy, jumped down, and checked the suspicious spots.

We looked for metallic mines with metal detectors, listening intently to each sound through the rustling in our earphones, knowing the price of the smallest mistake.

We drove our probes (long sticks with narrow metal ends) into the dirt roads, finding plastic mines by their hollow, dull sound.

I didn't learn to do this in boot camp; I learned to do it there. They ordered me to become minesweeper, and I became one.

"Minesweeper? Is that the one who lays the mines?" I was asked once.

"No, he's the one who gets blown away by them," I answered.

We could do anything, if necessary. Two minesweepers accompanied each group that went into the mountains, and there we became simple soldiers. But when necessary, we'd blow up what had to be blown up. Or we'd check the path, where there might be anti-personnel mines. Or we'd lay guided anti-personnel shrapnel mines to defend ourselves for the night. When necessary, I had to place two grenades in the dark such that they'd work from a thread stretched across the road. And then, the same night, I had to find them and remove them. I didn't know how to do it, but I learned, because it was necessary.

We checked the roads in front of the convoy.

We looked for mines, and we found them.

We did all this because we knew it was necessary—necessary for those who went behind us.

An English anti-transport mine, an MK-7. We had just found it, and it was still very dangerous. Some twenty meters away on this same road, I found another mine, and a short distance away, a third mine. But these were Italian mines, TS-6.1s. These were the first mines I found and disarmed.

A few hours later, when we returned from checking out the entire road, we passed the armored car that was first in line to go on that road, the car that was ready to roll, just a few meters away from the first mine I found. The driver came up to me and shook my hand and thanked me. He said that he'd had a mine explode on him once, and that once was enough to last his whole lifetime.

SEPTEMBER 5, 1985   PAGMAN, AFGHANISTAN

This was the first mine I ever found. The other minesweepers had already checked this road, but Oleg Palich, our commander, ordered us to check it again. In a few minutes, my probe knocked up against a rock. The sound was not completely ordinary—a little hollow. I dug up the rock and threw it away. But the probe knocked up against another rock. I started to dig it up, but instead of a rock, the ribbed, yellow edge of an "Italian" appeared in the dust. At that moment, one of the minesweepers who had checked the road before was going back down the road. When he saw the mine, he looked me in the eye and asked, "Which one?"

"The first."

"Do you need any help?"

"I'll do it myself."

"Good luck..."

"Sure!" I thought, sincerely.

A minesweeper has to work alone on a mine he finds—even if it explodes, the others will still have to check the road ahead. A minute later, the two of us were the only ones left on the road: the mine and me, one on one.

This deep crater is all that remains of my first mine. For the next three hours, we continue to check the road. Sergei Skoblikov will find another mine. It will also be the first in his life, while I will be up to my second. Three craters will remain behind us on the road. Tired, but happy, we will return to our armored transport, where the guys are already preparing a holiday dinner for us.

War is humdrum, just difficult, hard work. But we had our holidays, too. On this day I passed my minesweeping exam. Had I failed, I might have paid for it with a life, my own or that of someone who followed behind me.

On this day, I gave myself an exam . . . and passed it.

My commander. We called him simply Oleg Palich. This photograph was taken the day after the preceding photo. Palich often had premonitions of danger, especially in regard to mines. That is exactly what happened the day before. He'd been ordered to move our transport column down the road as fast as possible. But he had a premonition, and even though the road had already been checked by other minesweepers, he gave the order for us to check it again.

We used to get angry at him when, back at base, instead of letting us rest or watch TV, he made us get out in the dirt and check the road right under our windows. To our surprise, we found mines. As it turned out, they were training mines he himself had planted on the road, early in the morning while we were asleep. And these "jokes" made us even angrier at him. All the drivers knew that there couldn't be mines on that road, because it was on the base. Once, one of the drivers saw us deactivating a mine, and he screeched to a halt. He jumped out of his car and ran back to us, his eyes popping out of his head, and he asked, "What, there are even mines here, on base?"

Only when I came home did I understand that it was thanks to Oleg Palich that the majority of us made it home alive and whole.

This is a picture of Sergei Chudopalov. Often, he was not taken along on combat missions. The guys went into the mountains, and Sergei—he had beautiful
handwriting—was left on the base to write up stupid, unnecessary paperwork.
But soon he found an escape: he wrote at night and managed to finish all his
work before the combat missions. And then they let him go into the mountains. He was one of those who could not stay put when others were going to a
place from which they might not return.

In my hands is a mine, a MON-50 made in the USSR.

In the morning, they brought us in by helicopter, but we had to wait for days before the other troops came. The Mujahadeen were everywhere, and we had no choice but to spend the night here. We knew how many men we had, but we didn't know how many they had. That's why I left this mine on the trail for the night.

The MON-50 is a directional shrapnel mine. It destroys the living force of the enemy for a radius of approximately 60 degrees for a distance of up to 150 feet.

I set the mine so that it would be exploded by a detonating device. The wires were too short, and the second minesweeper in my team and I spent the night about forty yards from the trail, closer than anyone else. We took turns sleeping in two-hour shifts. All night a bright moon traitorously shed its light on us. The long shadows of the rocks blacked out the trail. Each two hours seemed an eternity. Until morning, barely visible sparks flashed dimly all around our small camp. The Mujahadeen were looking for us. We could even hear their voices.

. . . We stepped outside to smoke. She lived in a small wooden house on the outskirts of a little town not far from Moscow. "Let's go for a walk," she suggested, and we went out to the road. The bright moon shone at our backs. The long shadows of the trees blacked out the trail. Something heavy tugged at my heart. "No!" I answered rudely and walked back quickly. Barely visible sparks started to flash all over the place . . . I even heard *their* voices.

THE BASE

We believed that we still could believe. We knew there was much we didn't want to know. We tried to understand what was impossible to understand. And we even wanted what we had no right to want. Somewhere far behind, we'd crossed the line; there was no way back.

Freedom! I could sleep as much as I wanted, but it was a shame to waste time—I wanted to revel in this freedom. I jumped out of bed and went into the kitchen. Koozia ran in after me and lazily yawned. He began to meow pitifully, rubbing his head against my leg. It was hard to believe that he hadn't forgotten me in the last two years. For that, I had to feed him. Mama came up behind me and wrapped her arms around me, as if checking: was it really me or not? Yes, it was me. Alive and well. It was as hard for her to believe as it was for me. For a whole eternity I'd been waiting for this day, dreaming about it. In dreams I'd seen this morning, my first morning *home*. The tea kettle whistled.

"Good morning, son," said Mama, stroking my hair.

"Good morning," I answered and took the kettle off the stove.

For some reason, I couldn't look her in the eye.

As if regaining her senses, Mama began to bustle about, setting the table. But no matter what she was doing, she kept reaching out to touch me, as if making sure it wasn't a dream.

"Lemon?" she asked unexpectedly, pouring the tea. I winced. "Fucking Panjsher," I thought to myself, not answering.

"So, how are you?" she asked and sat down beside me, smiling happily and trying to look into my eyes.

"Later! OK?" I answered, staring stupidly into my cup. The lemon scent hit me. I wanted to cry, but I'd forgotten how.

. . . "Let them be quick," he said quietly, staring fixedly at the sky. Blood had seeped through the bandages on his chest, and I had to change them. I took out a new bandage, but he stopped me with his hand: "Do you hear? It's the copters!"

I listened intently...he was right. A few minutes later, the helicopters were circling above us, looking for a landing site.

"Don't be scared; you'll make it," I tried to encourage him. But he didn't hear me—he'd lost consciousness again.

Two days later, we returned to the base. Our supply sergeant met us near the entrance to the barracks. The company I'd gone out with was one of the last to get back, and it seemed one of the guys from my company had turned me in: Savchenko, the supply sergeant, was too happy to see me. He was basically a soldier like us, only too smart and too cunning. He never went out on combat missions, though occasionally officers took him along on the support convoys (he was a good cook). On base, his responsibilities were to keep our company room spick-and-span, to issue us weapons and uniforms (and count them), and to inform on us to the officers. He performed all these tasks splendidly, and therefore the officers protected him from veteran soldiers, whose tradition it was to humiliate the "green" soldiers and to force them to do the dirtiest work on base. Often the veteran soldiers would simply tell the supply sergeant what they needed, and he in turn would order the "greens" to fix them a snack, or run to the commissary, or launder their uniforms. The guys who had been drafted at the same time as Savchenko tried to stay away from him. Some simply kissed his ass. Others were afraid of him and did what he told them to. If they refused, he could put them on punishment detail— mopping floors and standing guard duty half the night, on only four hours sleep. (He could assign punishment detail for up to five days at a time, which left one no time to rest or get enough sleep before a combat mission.) A third group—like Oleg Loginov and Oleg Zaitsev—constantly went into the mountains on combat missions and never did anything wrong on base, or, if they did, they did it so no one would know. Savchenko tried not to touch them.

I was among those who were afraid of him, or, more precisely, I was afraid of his power to create horrible living conditions for me. Unfortunately, I was a sergeant with more responsibilities, and it was easy for him to pick on me. Then, too, I always took pity on my soldiers, letting them get more rest than they were supposed to. And when I became a veteran soldier (after one year in Afghanistan), I didn't bother the "greens," for which I lost a lot of respect—what kind of a veteran was I if I didn't hassle them?

Life on the base was bad enough, but Savchenko had the power to make it far worse. Often I requested combat duty just to get away from him . . .

. . . He met us near the barracks and smiled too widely, "You're back, are you," he grinned, slapping me on the shoulder, "at long last!"

It didn't look good for me. I wished there'd be some emergency, just so I could get away. Walking down the hall to our company room, my thoughts were racing: What could he have found out about? I decided it was the huge tub of butter that I'd sold over the fence to some Afghans, right before I left for combat. In general, the Afghans bought everything from us, everything from socks to tank engines. With our fine salary of ten rubles a month, we sold stuff often.

Where would we spend the money? Mostly on food. Army food was so bad that we tried to buy extra food in the commissary, or from Afghans themselves. We also tried to buy presents for our parents, right before going home. Sometimes we even bought cheap porno magazines—we weren't allowed to be with women in Afghanistan; after all we were soldiers, not human beings. And we weren't allowed to have any alcohol, not even beer. And we weren't allowed to go into the city, and we weren't allowed any military leaves to go home. Only those whose mother or father had died were allowed to go back for two weeks, and not always even then.

. . . For one fucking tub of butter, Savchenko put me on punishment detail that very day, not giving me a chance to rest after the mission. I could just forget about getting enough sleep. So, while everyone else slept, I went outside to get some fresh air. A soldier buddy from a neighboring company sat down beside me and lit up. I recognized the familiar smell of hashish.

"You want some?" he asked.

"Why not," I shrugged and immediately took a deep drag.

Speaking honestly, I don't remember anyone who didn't at least try the stuff. It wasn't hard to do: there was no problem getting drugs in Afghanistan. You could get a few grams of hash just by giving a pair of socks or a tin of fish to the little Afghan kids who hung around our fence. Naturally, some of us became addicted, but not that many. Most of us smoked only when we felt really bad about something (usually about everything).

. . . A few minutes later, the copters were circling above us, looking for a landing site. He came to and, catching sight of them, smiled unexpectedly: "Now, I'll make it."

The radioman was descending toward us, shouting something. I didn't like it. Running up, he pulled me aside: "The copters are scared to land. They say it's not safe. And for the sake of one wounded, they don't want to risk it."

Fortunately, he didn't hear anything—he'd lost consciousness again. He's not going to make it now, I thought, and squeezed his hand.

Freedom? It's a "conscious necessity." That's what they taught us in school, in college, in the army. They taught us, and they tried to make us live by this strange slogan. But I never could understand: do they really believe what they say? Most likely, they themselves no longer believed in anything, the same way that I no longer believed any of them.

This is a page from my Afghan notebook. This little scrap of paper meant so much to me, *there*.

The first column: the date.

The second column: how many days I'd served.

The third column: how many days I'd served in Afghanistan.

The fourth column: how many days I had left to serve.

The fifth column: how many days I had left to serve until the *next* semiannual demobilization order (we called it the Order). After *that* Order, it meant I'd have only six months left till *my* Order.

The sixth column: how many hours I had left to serve.

The seventh column: how many hours I had to serve till the next Order.

The eighth column: how many weeks I had to serve till the next Order, after which I'd have only half a year left to serve... six months... twenty-six weeks... one hundred eighty-one days... four thousand three hundred twenty hours. Each one of these hours could have cost me my life.

Числ/дс	отгл. дн.	АФИ дн.	ост. Σ	ост. Σ	ост. ч. Σ	ост. Σ	ост. нед Σ
1.V.8	384	280	314	133	7536	3192	
.V.8	382	284	310	129	7458	3076	
11.VI.8	409	305	289	108	6.934	2572	16
15.VII.8	413	309	285	104	6838	2516	15
17.VII.8	415	311	283	102	6790	2440	15
18.VII.8	416	312	282	101	6766	2424	15
24.VII.8	422	318	276	95	6622	2280	14
25.VII.8	423	319	275	94	6598	2256	14
3.VIII.8	431	327	264	86	6.406	2.064	13
6.VIII.85	434	330	264	83	6.336	1.992	12
7.VIII.85	435	331	263	82	6.312	1.968	12
8.VIII.85	436	332	262	81	6.288	1.944	12
1.VIII.8	460	306	238	57			
21.VIII.8	480	376	218	37	3232	888	
25.VIII.8	484	380	214	33	3136	792	6
14.IX.85	504	400	196	13	—		
19.IX.85	507	403					
10.X.85	531	427	169	—			

war

BAD

1985   KABUL, AFGHANISTAN

This shot was taken on the base. On our base, where instead of resting between combat missions, we practiced marching in formation. Our base, where the ones who took orders never returned, while their medals went to those who gave the orders. Our base, where kind people were transformed into vicious ones. Where the vicious became cruel. Where they made boys into murderers. For what? In the background of this picture, part of a slogan is visible: "To Afghan-Soviet Friendship." It was a strange sort of friendship. And no less strange a price we paid for it.

1985 KABUL, AFGHANISTAN

On holidays, the local Afghan party bigwigs often came to see us. On those days there were lots of journalists around, both Soviets and Afghans. They asked us very few questions, and they were afraid to look us in the eye. Their assignment was simple—to snap several appropriately cheerful pictures and to write several equally cheerful lines. Only in this picture I see something else; I hear different music. Because I know that at this moment, this orchestra is playing neither a festive march nor a glorifying hymn. It is playing honest music, in memory of those who have been killed.

This is an exhibit of weapons confiscated during one of our operations. Reporters came to see us and to photograph the weapons. Then they left. Not one of them wrote about the fact that the high-caliber machine gun, the DShK, in the background was made in the USSR. In the 1930s and 1940s the Soviet Union still supplied China with arms. And in the 1980s these arms turned up in Afghanistan. With these machine guns the Mujahadeen shot down our helicopters; under their fire our boys were killed.

We captured the DShKs and gave them to the Afghan government forces, which often sold them back to the Mujahadeen. And the cycle again repeated itself, as if our lives and fates were being broken apart in some kind of eternal meat grinder. In which our own weapons fired at us.

Many of them came to Afghanistan, played at toy soldiers, received medals, and left. When I was little, I liked to play at toy soldiers too; only my soldiers were toys. It's a pity that these generals forget that their toys are flesh-and-blood people.

I call such generals "old children." And sometimes it scares me that these "children" may someday be playing with the red button.

These decorations and medals will be presented in a few minutes. Within these small pieces of metal is the blood of our friends, the pain of our hearts. Life and death, anguish and despair, have all been poured into them. So the war was doomed, so it was pointless. Still, we soldiers in this war did what we could, as best we could. We gave our lives not for the sake of somebody's illusory goals, not for the sake of distorted ideals, but for the sake of those who were standing behind us. For the sake of those who ate from the same mess-tin. For the sake of those who, without hesitation, would do the same for us. In these decorations are the lives of those who died, and the pain of those who returned.

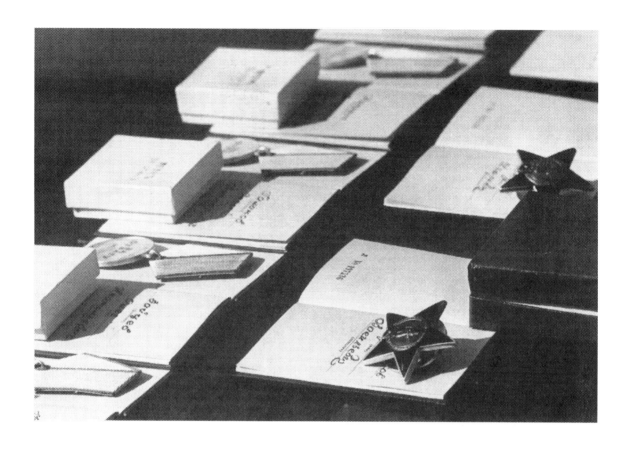

This wreath is lying at the foot of a memorial to Soviet boys who were killed in Afghanistan.

On this wreath is the following inscription, in capital letters: "From the grateful people of Afghanistan."

1985 KABUL, AFGHANISTAN

This monument to "soldiers fulfilling their international duty" was built on our base in 1985. Soviet television announced the ceremonial unveiling with these words, "This monument will become the symbol of Afghan-Soviet friendship."

We felt differently about it. For us it was a giant gravestone. For us it was a symbol of revenge. We took revenge on *them* for our friends who remained here forever. *They* took revenge on us for their brothers who fell after our friends. And the longer we were here, the more vicious this circle became. And that was the true symbolism of this monument.

IN COUNTRY

It had a rather banal beginning. In December 1979 Soviet troops entered Afghanistan. This wasn't anything unusual; our troops were already in East Germany, Poland, Czechoslovakia, Hungary; sometimes they dropped in on Africa, and even briefly on Egypt. So one country more or one country less—it didn't make much difference.

It's only now, after the Soviet government has officially declared *it was a mistake to bring Soviet troops into Afghanistan,* only now that the Soviet press has started to write *it was a mistake to bring Soviet troops into Afghanistan.* But at the time, *Soviet troops entered Afghanistan at the request of the Afghan people to bring comradely help to our Great Neighbor,* our government announced. *At the request of the Afghan people, in order to bring comradely help to our Great Neighbor, Soviet troops entered Afghanistan,* our newspapers said, and they printed pictures of smiling Soviet soldiers surrounded by laughing Afghan children.

On August 10, 1984, my plane landed in Kabul, the capital of Afghanistan. There were no skyscrapers there. The blue domes of the mosques and the faded mountains were the only things rising above the adobe *duvals* (the houses). The mosques came alive in the evening with multivoiced wailing: the mullahs were calling the faithful to evening prayer. It was such an unusual spectacle that, in the beginning, I used to leave the barracks to listen—the same way that, in Russia, spring nights, people go outside to listen to the nightingales sing. For me, a nineteen-year-old boy who had lived his whole life in Leningrad, everything about Kabul was exotic: enormous skies—uncommonly starry—occasionally punctured by the blazing lines of tracers. And spread out before you, this mysterious Asian capital where strange people were bustling about like ants in an anthill: bearded men, faces darkened by the sun, in solid-colored wide cotton trousers and long shirts. Their modern

jackets, worn over those outfits, looked completely unnatural. And women, hidden under plain dull garments that covered them from head to toe; only their hands visible, holding bulging shopping bags, and their feet, in worn-out shoes or sneakers, sticking out from under the hems.

And somewhere between this odd city and the deep black southern sky, the wailing, beautifully incomprehensible songs of the mullahs. The sounds didn't contradict each other, but rather, in a polyphonic echo, melted away among the narrow streets. The only thing missing was Scheherazade with her tales of *A Thousand and One Arabian Nights*... A few days later I saw my first missile attack on Kabul. This country was at war.

The war divided the Afghan people. Some were with us, and others were against us. On our side was the Afghan government, which had come to power in April 1978 (not without our help), and the Afghan Republican Army. This army, like any other, was made up of officers and soldiers. Most officers received special training at Afghan military colleges; some even studied in the Soviet Union. An "amusing" example of this kind of training: an Afghan officer named Ahmad Shah. He had graduated from a Soviet military academy, returned to Afghanistan, and went over to the Mujahadeen in Panjsher, where he headed one of their largest groups and put his training to good use. Actually, the only thing an Afghan had to do to enter a military college was apply, and he was in. They chose the soldiers differently: troops went into a village and rounded up men of appropriate age. There were some volunteers, of course—a few.

The Afghan army often took part in combat missions together with Soviet troops. Frankly, they were lousy soldiers. They tried to stay behind us and were never in a hurry to overtake us. There was nothing surprising about this: many of them, like many of us, were not in this war of their own free will. We had nothing to lose but our lives, but they were fighting their *own* people on their *own* land. Our newspapers depicted them as brave and valiant warriors defending their revolution. There were some volunteers who fought on our side to avenge the deaths of their families murdered by the Mujahadeen. Just as there were those who fought on the side of the Mujahadeen to avenge the death of families killed by our shelling. This is what a civil war is about. The only question was, What were *we* doing there? And why were there more and more unmarked graves in *our* cemeteries?

. . . We stood silently at the Vietnam Wall.

"There's always a lot of people in Washington on this day," John said unexpectedly, and started to walk away.

"Today is Memorial Day," explained his wife, Melanie, as she went to catch up with him. Reaching him, she carefully took his arm in hers. They walked away like that. Together. Silently. I walked behind them, and the endless names flashed by me, etched in black stone.

"How many of yours were killed?" Melanie asked, stopping.

"Officially, fifteen thousand," I answered.

"And unofficially?"

"I think two or three times more than that," I took out a cigarette.

"You can't smoke here," John reminded me, and we went to the car. On the way home, he picked up a few movies for the evening. "This is for you," he said, handing me a videotape.

"Rambo in Afghanistan!" Melanie smiled. "You'll find that interesting."

The film turned out to be quite amusing. A well-done cheap action picture. And here are the Mujahadeen: their tired, worn-out faces, heads held high. It was easy to see: they were defending their land and families from Soviet soldiers. "Is that true?" asked Melanie, hitting the pause button.

Yes, it was partly right. At home, in the Soviet Union, they showed only the villages burned by the Mujahadeen and newsreel footage of them shooting down civilian aircraft. From that point of view, our television and newspapers were also partly right. As for me, I can only talk about what I saw.

I saw houses burned by the Mujahadeen, as well as disfigured bodies of prisoners they'd taken. But I saw other things too: villages destroyed by our shelling and bodies of women, killed by mistake. When you shoot at every rustling in the bushes, there's no time to think about who's there. But for an Afghan, it didn't matter if his wife had been killed intentionally or accidentally. He went into the mountains to seek revenge.

So Afghans became Mujahadeen in different ways. From my point of view, there were three kinds of Mujahadeen.

The first, and the largest number of them, were Afghans who simply went to work to earn money from the war. The majority of these received special training in the Peshawar region of Pakistan. To "do their job" they used American Stingers and M-16 rifles, Italian and English mines, and Chinese automatics (unsuccessful copies of Soviet Kalashnikovs). In a word, they had no problems obtaining weapons. For their work, they were paid regularly: from 5,000 to 10,000 afghanis for killing a Soviet soldier; from 10,000 to 20,000 for killing a Soviet officer; about 100,000 for destroying a tank or a helicopter or an airplane. An example: once three Mujahadeen were captured in the mountains. They turned out to be Afghan students who were attending Soviet universities. They'd come home for summer vacation and decided to earn some extra money. Among other things, war is a business. Someone sells weapons, someone uses them.

We usually called the Mujahadeen by the less impressive word *Dushman* ("bandit"). The Dushmans were in the mountains long before the war, only there weren't so many. They stole a bit and dealt in drugs a little, when suddenly the opportunity arose to have a "stable income." There was competition for these jobs. We often heard about fighting between neighboring groups of Mujahadeen; the issue was territorial control.

Journalists don't write about these Mujahadeen in the foreign (and that includes the "free" American) press. But they write about them constantly in the Soviet press.

The second kind of Mujahadeen are the ones who took up arms to defend their country from us. They don't care whether the troops are Soviet, American, or Martian. Any alien who comes into their land bearing weapons is their enemy. I respected these Afghans, although we were on opposite sides of the barricades. The foreign press wrote a lot about them; the Soviet press diligently ignored them.

The third kind were those who went into the mountains not of their own choosing. Mujahadeen came into their villages, threatening to destroy everything, and took away the men. They needed more men, and if they hadn't taken these men, the Afghan Republican Army would in time have come and taken them.

But it would be untrue to say all Afghans were involved in the war. Many of them, simple peasants, harvested their crops, herded their sheep, and fed their families. If the war got too close, they were precisely the ones who were in the worst position. Many of them were forced to leave their land—some fled to the mountains, some to Pakistan, some to Iran. But some of them chose another way. For example, when our troops came to the Bamian region, several elders came out to meet us. In the name of all the inhabitants of the surrounding villages, they gave our troops an ultimatum. It was a simple ultimatum: "We aren't hiding any Mujahadeen. We are peaceful peasants, who have worked on this land all our lives. And if the Mujahadeen come, we can defend ourselves. We won't let them in. And we won't let you in either. We don't want deaths here. But if you come on our land with weapons, we will defend ourselves."

It may sound strange, but we believed them. We believed them, and we left. We knew they were telling the truth, and we didn't want the deaths of our soldiers any more than they wanted the deaths of their people. Somewhere in our subconscious, we understood that the only thing we wanted was to go home. We also knew that if someone invaded our land, we would defend ourselves, just as these Afghans were doing. That's how it was for Napoleon in Russia, for Hitler in the Soviet Union, for the Americans in Vietnam, and for us in Afghanistan.

1985   KABUL, AFGHANISTAN

The center of Kabul looked like a normal modern city. The same kinds of people. The same students with their schoolbooks. The same women, in normal dresses, not in those shapeless garments. In the center of Kabul there were taxis, trolleybuses, universities. It would appear that the city was leading a normal life, if not for . . .

If not for the Soviet armored personnel carriers on the streets.

If not for the sharp shouts of the Afghan patrols at night. "Halt!"

If not for the regular rocket attacks.

If not for, if not for, if not for . . . if not for the war.

Catching sight of our convoy, this Afghan turned off the road at once. Usually, we were given the right of way . . . during daylight.

On the outskirts of Kabul, Afghans reacted to us in different ways. The old men smiled widely at us, or simply turned their heads away. But the young ones—they always looked us right in the eye.

We spent a few days not far from this house. A huge family lived there, and it was clear they were very poor. What we couldn't understand was why they had three camels lying in their yard, each one of which cost a fortune by Afghan standards. But we had an unspoken agreement with them: they gave us clean, fresh water from their well, and we didn't ask them how they got their camels.

In this picture, I'm twenty years old. Before this, I'd seen camels only in the zoo, and in a cage at that. And here—a live, big, dusty one, bending his head toward me, like a cat, for me to pet. To this day, I remember the feel of his warm, shaggy neck under my hand.

Exactly one week before this picture was taken, I was also twenty. Until then, I'd seen Mujahadeen only far away, and then only in the sights of my gun. But that day—a live one, real, with trembling arms raised above his head.

According to the rules of war, I should have taken him prisoner. But there were no rules in this war. I had no choice—there were only three of us, and we didn't know how many of them were left.

To this day, I remember the fear in his eyes; it was so strong, that it was hard for me to take aim. All I could do was close my eyes and pull the trigger.

OCTOBER 1985   KABUL PROVINCE, AFGHANISTAN

For several days we had been guarding a road. We were high in the mountains, and our food ran out.

Every morning we got water from a small river close to this house. The morning I took this picture, we went up to the house and asked the people if we could have some bread. One woman went into the house and came out with flour. And there, right in front of us, she mixed the dough and baked us bread.

And when I held that hot, fragrant bread in my hands, I almost forgot that somewhere right close by, there was a war.

Memories of the Future

The photos I took in Afghanistan are lying in front of me. I peer into the faces of those who were with me there and who are so far away from me now, into the faces of those who were dying right next to me and those who were hiding behind my back. I can make these photos larger or smaller, darker or lighter. But there's nothing I can do to erase the shadow of misery and despair from the eyes looking back at me from the photos. How often I run across these eyes in the streets here, now. And, involuntarily, I ask myself, "How many of us were there? And how many were left there forever?"

We were all different when we got there and all different when we came back. But something in common has shown up that unites us and that cannot be shared with others. Maybe it is our memories, which make us wake up in a cold sweat at night. Maybe it is the blood on our hands, which does not give us a minute's peace day or night. I don't know, and I am afraid to think about it. But I just don't want to see those who were *there* with me anymore. Because *here* they have already become different, strangers to me. And I won't be able to forgive them this betrayal, just as I can't forgive myself. I am afraid to see the change in those who shared their last crust of bread with me, who shielded me in battle, who helped me when I couldn't move anymore, and whom I helped when it was worse for them than for me. I am afraid to lose them. Maybe they are all that is left to me.

At first I didn't understand that. So when I returned, I invited one of them to my wedding. He arrived, and I ran to the station so I could see him that much sooner.

He had been wounded in Panjsher. An exploding bullet entered his heel and splintered his leg. I heard on the walkie-talkie that somebody was badly wounded in his company. I don't know why, but I sensed that it was him. And when they were passing us a few hours later, I saw that they were carrying

someone lying on his back. They were far away and it was impossible to see who it was, but I already knew that it was him.

I ran up to the train and spotted him immediately. He was standing with his wife. She was noticeably pregnant and all the time he had to shield her with his outstretched arm from the people who were hurrying to their trains. At that moment I realized that I didn't want to see him anymore, not the way he was now.

He was my best friend in that other life. But here, two strangers met at the station. We shared a common past. What we lived on *there* was our faith in the future, at least our faith that we would have a future. And as the future became the present, the present had become the past, standing face-to-face we probably both understood that there was nothing between us except memories. Memories are where the past merges with the future.

Could it have been otherwise? There is a mixture of good and evil in all of us. Life doesn't change us. It changes only the balance of these forces. There are no evil people; there are simply people in whom there is more evil than good. There are no honest people; there are simply people who tell the truth. But who knows, perhaps tomorrow it will be a lie. We lived our first eighteen years with our own truth. We imbibed it with our mothers' milk. They taught it to us at school. We heard it on the radio and saw it on television. We read it in the newspaper, and we said it to each other. But we found ourselves *there*, and we had to start all over again. Because of the war, good and evil changed places *there*. We learned to kill in order to live, to fall in order to rise, to die in order to become eternal. And that was also the truth, but it was the truth for another life, for the one we were living *there*. Because war is also life, but with its own laws. And we had only one choice to make: either to live by these laws or to die. But one could live by them in different ways, and everyone made his own choice.

Letters meant a lot to us, maybe even too much. They were the only thing that linked us with that other world, which we couldn't forget, which lived inside us, to which we dreamed of returning. They were our hope, our faith in the fact that it would all come to an end and that it was possible to live differently.

...He was walking a bit ahead of me. He was reeling terribly, but by some miracle he managed to stay on his feet. Everything about him was disgusting: his dirty, crumpled suit, his slightly gray, long, unwashed hair, and his hairy legs as they shuffled along in his filthy, broken-down boots. Yet he was no more than twenty years old. His hands kept pushing the crowd away as people streamed by him. I ran past him and looked back to make sure that he appeared no less offensive from the front than from the back. Suddenly, the blue medal ribbon pin caught my eye. I knew only too well what it meant. We paid too high a price to get that medal. A medal "For Valor."

...I finished reading the last letter. We had just come back to the base and there was almost no one in the barracks. Some guys were cleaning their weapons. Others ran to the bathhouse. The rest were asleep already. Sergei was sitting right across from me. I didn't like him. He was too vicious. I didn't like that type. But then I noticed how carefully and tenderly he was tracing the first line of his letter: "Greetings, Dearest Grandma..."

...There were oranges at the grocery store, and I joined the line for some. It was a short line, only about five people. It was early morning and a calm, even lazy, atmosphere ruled the shop. A fellow came straight up to the counter. I thought, "What nerve! He's cutting in front." A boy of seventeen, who looked rather athletic, was at the front of the line. He said something to the fellow through clenched teeth. The old women behind him joined in and began to scold halfheartedly. In a flash, the guy turned around and shoved a certificate under the boy's nose. "Here, look. I have the right. I spilled blood in Afghanistan while you were here..."

..."Greetings, Dearest Grandma." I wouldn't have believed that he could write such words. Opposing feelings struck me. After all, I had known him to be quite different. I remembered his fury when he had pulled a green recruit who had tried to evade action from the aid station. I remembered the hatred with which he beat him with the back of his hand and screamed, "You're afraid, you little shit! And when you get home you're going to tell girls fairy tales about Afghanistan and bang your chest with your fist!" I had seen a fury in his eyes when we fell into an ambush. He was ecstatic when he shot down an Afghan from Pakistan who was trying to escape. I remembered all that and I couldn't believe that he had another side, that something human was left in him. Three weeks later, Sergei was killed.

...I loved her, but with him she knew what would happen tomorrow. With me she couldn't even guess what had happened yesterday. I popped up unexpectedly and vanished the same way. But when I came back to be with her forever, she wasn't there anymore. She was too tired. It was calmer with him—she had made her choice. It was too difficult for her to understand why I had changed. What prevents me from staying in one place and won't give me a minute's peace?

... Three weeks later Sergei was killed. He was blown up by a mine; they said there was almost nothing left of him. In a month his brother came to us. Though he served somewhere nearby, he hadn't managed to visit us before. There was so much "work" to do. A master sergeant came up to me and said, "He doesn't know anything. Will you say something?" He said that and went to bed. But what could I say? And what for? I took Sergei's photo down from the wall and gave it to his brother. It was in a black frame. We spent an hour, maybe more, sitting together in silence. I didn't know one could cry without tears. He said, "I didn't make it in time," and left.

The photos I took in Afghanistan are lying in front of me. I peer into the faces of those who were with me there and who are so far away from me now, into the faces of those who were dying right next to me and those who were hiding behind my back. I can make these photos larger or smaller, darker or lighter. But what I can't do is bring back those who are gone forever.

These two soldiers are from my platoon: Aleksei Godovnikov (left), and Oleshka Zaitsev (right). A few minutes from this moment, they'll be flying in helicopters toward the mountains. In forty minutes, people will be shooting at these nineteen-year-old boys. And they will shoot back, and they will kill. That is the law of war: if you don't kill first, they'll kill you. We didn't invent this law.

But having landed in a war, we have to live by its rules. And the quicker you learn these rules, the longer you have to live by them. You don't think about whether you are defending someone's revolution or defending the "southern borders of the motherland." You simply shoot at those who are shooting at you and at your friend behind you—you shoot at the guys whose mines blew away your friend yesterday.

These boys will return home alive. They will return home with war medals and concussions. They will think that Afghanistan has become part of their past.

By 1989, the total number of Vietnam veterans who had died in violent accidents or by suicide after the war exceeded the total number of American soldiers who died during the war.

I don't remember his name. I don't remember where he was from. I remember that our climb into the mountains was grueling, and we were exhausted. He was new. This was one of his first battles. I was more experienced and I wanted to encourage him, to cheer him up.

I gave a shout, to get his attention, and when he turned toward me, I took this picture. I teased him, saying now he'd have a picture to send home that showed he was alive and well.

But I doubt that he sent *this* picture home. Because we all tried to send pictures and letters that showed how healthy and rested we were, so as not to frighten our parents.

I used to write my parents that I was serving somewhere abroad, that I was eating grapes, reading a lot, and watching TV. But in my parents' first letter back to me, my father wrote that I shouldn't think they were stupid, that they knew perfectly well where I was.

When I came home two years later, I was shocked to see the change in my mother. She had gotten old.

Viktor Savchenko, my platoon's supply sergeant. Unlike many, he tried his best to get out of going on combat missions. He didn't even try to hide it.

Sergeant Savchenko was responsible for the general order and cleanliness of our platoon; he also ratted on us to the officers. He fulfilled his duties very well. In our barracks, everything was always neat and clean. Everything was always in its rightful place. And the officers were always well informed as to who was smoking dope, and how much.

Having ended up in the war, Savchenko decided to make the war his career. Though he never once made it to the mountains, he managed to come home with a military medal, the Red Star. (The Red Star is usually awarded posthumously to those who died in battle.)

I am sure that once he was safe at home, he beat his fist against his breast and shouted at every corner that he had spilled his blood in Afghanistan. Unfortunately, there were guys like him there. Not many, but there were some.

Sergei Matveyev is standing next to me. In Afghanistan he was my best friend. On this day we were resting up; the next day we were planning to go into the mountains again. He walked up to me and sat down beside me. We sat together for about an hour and then he said, "Let's go take our picture for a souvenir...together!" "What are you thinking about? What's happening?" I asked. "I don't know," he said, unsure of himself. Two days later, he was seriously wounded. An exploding bullet hit him in the heel and shattered his leg.

In our army, time served is measured not by years, but by Orders. Every six months, every September 26 and March 26, official Orders are issued, and soldiers who've finished serving their two years are eligible for demobilization. It's the custom, among our troops, to shave your head when you have only one Order (six months) left to serve.

When we woke up on September 26, we knew we had only one Order left to serve. Within a few hours, we were on our way to help one of our groups that had been ambushed.

I noticed him from far away. He was running, leaning on his automatic, shouting at me not to shoot, that he was ours. I recognized him, though not at first. We had often met on the base. Now he was covered in blood, which was dripping from a small hole in his chest. He said he'd been lying on the ground for over an hour, pretending to be dead. He had lost a lot of blood. While I unraveled his sweater and bandaged his chest, he kept trying to explain to me why he hadn't been able to help his friend. His friend had been killed because he'd tried immediately to crawl out from under the bullets.

He kept getting worse. He didn't take his eyes off the sky, and asked me to have the helicopter come as soon as possible. When the helicopter arrived and took him, I knew that he would die.

Five months later, I was taking a shower at the base. He appeared out of nowhere and offered to scrub my back for me. The first stupid question that popped out of my mouth was, "You're *alive?*" To which he answered, "No, I died a while ago."

Back then, I couldn't understand why he had returned to Afghanistan after being released from the hospital. They had wanted to send him home. But now I understand. There was too big a difference between the peaceful, quiet life back at home and our life here, where we knew the value of living.

Two years after I came home, I had the first dream in which I returned to Afghanistan. I was walking through the base, looking for familiar faces, the faces of my friends. But I couldn't find them. And it was painful for me when I awoke and understood that those people and that time could never be brought back.

Each one believed that he would return home, even though we knew that not all of us could return.

We dreamed about how, back home, we would be able to go walking in the forest without fear and without weapons; about how we wouldn't be afraid of the dark, or of sudden noises, or that we'd be blown up on the road.

I dreamed about this; I believed in these dreams. And I couldn't ever have imagined that it wouldn't be like that.

Very often I feel terror. I'm afraid to go in the forest by myself. I'm afraid of the bright moon, of dark bushes, of silence. I'm afraid to be alone. I'm afraid when someone is standing behind me. I'm afraid of hitting a person because I know that I could lose control and start to kill him.

And it's not because I am scared of dying; it's because I want to live.

Somebody Had to Be the First

Few of us were sent directly to Afghanistan. First we were sent for training at a military camp not far from the border. I don't know if I was lucky or not, but instead of half a year, I spent only three and a half months there. I was probably lucky. It was too hard to wait, to wait for the answer to the question *when*. Some, who couldn't wait for the answer, tried to escape. But they were caught, put on a plane, and sent to the front with everyone else. Some refused. But their mouths were shut for them, and they were also sent to the front with everyone else. It was all the same to me. I already understood that there was no way to change anything. Here, all decisions concerning me were made by others. Even at the beginning, the urgent dispatch of Soviet troops was called "the replacement of those who finished their active service before the appointed time." What did these words mean? They meant that new troops were being sent to replace the dead and the wounded, to replace those who were unlucky in this massacre. The massacre in which we defended "their revolution" from them, while they defended their land from us.

August 10, 1984. My first day in Afghanistan. There, on the other side of a fence is the strange, unknown country, the country where everything is alien to me. But somewhere in there is our "little regiment," as we called it. A little piece of home. Only the people are sort of different, with a strange, incomprehensible sadness and suspicion in their eyes. There were ten people present in my company. "The others are in the mountains," someone explained to me. They came back the next day. I met them at the entrance. Boys, much like myself, were walking toward me. But it seemed to me that they were much older than me. In their dusty, yellow faces there was nothing, nothing but fatigue. As he passed me, one of them remarked, "A greenhorn." I was offended, but glad that at least somebody had noticed me.

A week later, our company commander called everyone together. "Tomorrow morning we'll fight. We are short two men. Which of the green recruits wants to go?" I took a step forward. I wasn't brave, but I felt ashamed when I looked into the eyes of those who had returned from the mountains. I wanted to know, I had to know why they were unlike me.

I remember only fragments from that battle. I remember my "chief," Seryoga Artemyev, slowly lighting a cigarette and lazily explaining what we ought to do in case firing started nearby. I remember my company commander digging a foxhole with his bayonet in about one minute when a sniper "found" him. There was a call on the walkie-talkie: "We have three twenty-ones. We need help . . ."

Now I know that "three twenty-ones" means three new scraps of paper that read "Your son perished while fulfilling his . . ." Now I understand why Seryoga stuck one of the dead men with a little hole in his forehead right under my nose and yelled, "Look out and remember to stay down." Now I understand that somebody had to be the first to be killed and that somebody had to be the last. We didn't know *who* would be the first, but we knew that there had to be one.

The first was Aleksei Kondrashev. He was killed unexpectedly, for all of us. For eight months death had missed us. At a moment when we least expected it, it struck from behind. Aleksei was blown up by a mine. Nobody knows whose mine—it may even have been one of our own. Just before the battle, he had asked our company commander, "Am I going?"

"Do you really want to?"

"Yes, I do."

Aleksei was a little clumsy, but it was always interesting to talk with him, about everything. When he was killed, I got scared. I wasn't scared because I was afraid of death. I just realized that soon there would be a second.

Three weeks later, we were leaving for battle. Sasha Zaichenko came up to me and said, "You know, I'm afraid." I didn't understand him then.

When we were in Jalalabad I asked him, "Well, how are you?"

"Not so hot. You'd better snap me for a souvenir. I'll send a picture home . . . when we get back."

In a few hours, we were in the mountains. It wasn't clear whether we were running from death or it was running after us. The radio operator called to me, "Hey you, minesweeper! One of your guys is wounded. He was in an ambush!" When we returned to Kabul I already knew that Sasha Zaichenko had died in the hospital.

. . . I asked, "Well, how are you?" He answered, "Not so hot."

There was a TV set in our company. We could watch telecasts from the Soviet Union. We learned from them how many new schools had been built in Afghanistan by Soviet soldiers and exactly where Afghan government troops had successfully carried out the regular military operations. But we didn't have much time for watching TV, and there was no time to rejoice in these successes. Summer came and we spent our days mostly in the mountains. And the more often we went there, the fewer of us came back. Mostly modest, but cheerful lines appeared in the press about the successes of the Afghan Republican Army. It was like that before we came, and so it remained after we left. Nobody believed this war would come to an end. We understood this war would last forever. All we really wanted was to return home as soon as possible, to return alive and with our arms and legs. We did our best to make that happen, but it didn't always depend on us.

July 10, 1985. Everything was as usual. We were preparing for our routine operations, and nobody paid attention when a small group left our base to escort a motorcade. It was our regular duty, an almost daily task. In a few hours the escort group had returned. Everything seemed as usual, but something was wrong. As I approached our barracks, my feeling of anxiety grew with every step. At the entrance there were only two armored jackets instead of seven.

It was too much. Too painful, too terrible. And there inside was Volodya Krivich—dusty, dirty with blood. With trembling hands and terror in his eyes he tried to explain something to me. But he was stammering and he forgot the words. I shook him and tried to understand. Only it was too terrible to understand. Three of our minesweepers were blown up by one mine, two others were badly shell-shocked and were in the hospital. Volodya was shaking all over. Nobody knew then that he himself would be blown up by the same kind of mine within a year.

He also wanted to return home as soon as possible, alive, with his arms and legs. And he also tried to make the best of it. But our fate did not always depend on us.

"In July 1985 Afghan government troops carried out several successful operations in Afghanistan, the result of which . . ."

He was also nineteen years old. Sasha was my friend. He wanted to be a pilot; he wanted to fly. Right before a military operation, he asked me to write a letter home to my parents in Leningrad, requesting information about how to apply to the Leningrad Aviation Institute. During the skirmish, I found out he'd been killed. I knew this when we returned to our base. I knew it, but I couldn't believe it. It seemed to me as if he had simply gone away, gone home, or maybe he was lying in a hospital. I felt that he wasn't here among us, but surely he was alive, somewhere.

The next day came a letter back from my parents, in which they went on for four pages about the procedures for applying to flight school. I read the letter, thinking, No, this isn't what Sasha wants, this isn't the right place for him to study flying, there he won't learn to fly. And suddenly I understood that he didn't need to apply anywhere anymore, that he'd never learn to fly, because he simply wasn't anymore.

Like me, he was nineteen. But he didn't come home. He was killed twelve hours after this photo was taken.

On this morning, before we went into the mountains we gathered to eat breakfast together. But this time they went into the mountains and I remained at the camp. In order to assuage my "guilt," I photographed everyone right here at the table. My detail returned to the base about two days before the others, and I managed to print the pictures in one night. As always, I printed enough pictures for everyone who appeared in the photo. But when they came back, I was left with one too many pictures. Aleksei Kondrashev had been blown up by a mine; someone got something mixed up on the map, and the group walked across a minefield. Nobody knows whose mine it was. It may even have been ours.

Aleksei Kondrashev, nineteen years old. This was his last picture. He is in the very back, behind everyone else...

This nineteen-year-old boy was killed in battle. He covered his commanding officer, Lieutenant Ivonin, with his own chest, and took the bullets that were intended for the officer.

This drawing of Aleksandr was done from memory by the officer whose life he saved. Posthumously, Aleksandr Koryavin was awarded the highest medal, the Gold Star. He was also named a Hero of the Soviet Union. The Gold Star was ceremoniously given to his mother, in place of her living son.

Most of us came home. Only we all came home differently. Some of us on crutches, some of us with gray hair, many in zinc coffins.

What did this war give us? Thousands of mothers who lost sons, thousands of cripples, thousands of torn-up lives. War made me grow up fast, but it made me old for my years.

It made me an old young man.

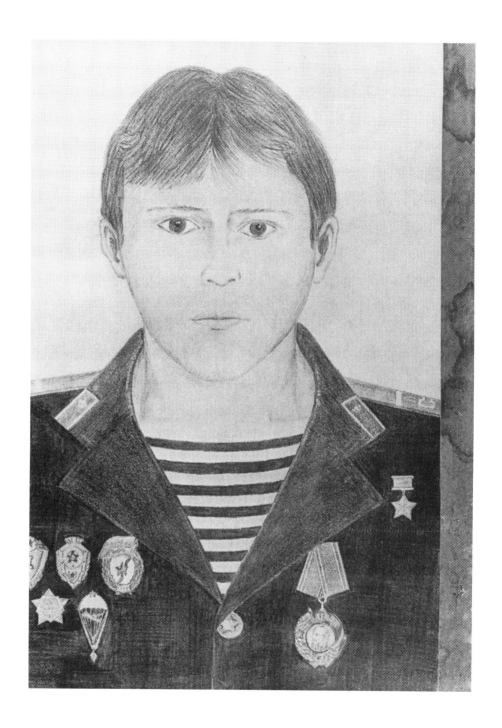

The officers tried to protect those who had little time left to serve before going home. Too often, right after a letter that told them "Wait for me! I'll be home soon," parents received a zinc coffin.

Kravchenko was down to his last few months, and the company commanders tried not to send him into the mountains. But some "greens" were sent to us, and he went out with them to check a road—he was training them. He was training them so that they would return home in a year and a half. They would return home alive. With arms. With legs. But he didn't have time. On July 10, 1985, with three months left before his return home, while he was checking a road, he was blown up by a mine. He was blown up instead of one of them.

MAY 1985   KABUL, AFGHANISTAN   VLADIMIR KRIVICH

Whenever a group of soldiers went up into the mountains they took two mine-sweepers along. During this engagement, I was paired with Volodya. He was still "green"—this was his first foray into the mountains—but he learned fast, and the main thing was you could depend on him. In the mountains, it is always clear who is who. The war peels people's shells off. The war taught me not to believe words, only actions.

When I came home, Volodya still had six months to serve. I corresponded with him, but after two months he stopped answering my letters, and I was offended. I stopped writing to him.

Two years later I learned that he had been blown up by a mine.

It was always hard for him to remain on the base while others went up into the mountains on combat missions, because he couldn't look them in the eye when they came back.

I held this photo in my hands and didn't know what I wanted to say about it. Then I understood that I should say nothing about it. The indifferent numbers tell it all.

Oleg Loginov. On the left, nineteen years old. One month ago, he got his second concussion. In forty-six days he will get his third, the most serious. He will spend one month in the hospital, but will return to our company all the same.

Renat Mukhamadiev. Second from the left, nineteen years old. In forty-six days a mine will explode several feet from him. The force of the explosion will hurl him so hard that only by chance will he survive.

Aleksandr Zaichenko. Third from the left, nineteen years old. In fourteen hours, on May 25, 1985, he will be killed in an ambush.

Vladimir Krivich. Second from the right, nineteen years old. In forty-six days three minesweepers will be blown up by one mine several yards away from him. And in one year he will be killed by the explosion of the same kind of mine.

Sergei Zaitsev. On the right, twenty years old. In forty-six days, on July 10, 1985, while testing a road, Sergei will find a mine. When he starts to defuse it, the mine will explode. A minesweeper makes mistakes once...

THE CIRCLE—A SYMBOL OF ETERNITY

We didn't believe in God, though we often thought of him. We were not afraid of death, though we encountered it constantly. We got to know the slapping sound a bullet makes when it hits a body. We grew to understand how short the step from life to death can be. We have a lot to remember, but we don't want to remember it. We have nothing to be proud of. There was something insane about it all. Maybe everything about it was insane. And the closer we were to coming home—the longer we had stayed there—the more unbearable it all became, and the sooner we wanted to return home. As I was flying back to Leningrad, I couldn't believe that for me, the war was coming to an end. My body became unusually soft and weak when I was struck by the thought, "That's it. It's all over."

"But it turned out that it wasn't all over," Jack said, walking to the window. A gray, sticky autumn rain covered the city. Only a few taxi drivers had stuck around the entrance of the hotel. Not far from the cruiser *Aurora,* a few workers were trying to put back in place the wind-torn banner with the slogan LONG LIVE THE GREAT OCTOBER. The city was getting ready to celebrate the seventy-first anniversary of the Soviet state. Jack drew the blind, sat on the edge of the table, and went on. "When we returned, they treated us like murderers. Nobody asked us if we wanted to serve in Vietnam—at that time our army was not an all-volunteer force. Everyone wondered *what* we were doing there, but not *why* we were there."

It was a little different with us. People went to see us off, but there weren't many waiting for us when we got back. While we were there, our girlfriends were getting married and our parents' hair was turning prematurely gray. While we were getting killed, our newspapers were announcing that we were planting trees and building schools. While the Soviet armed forces were sending in new recruits, the troops were sending out the dead and wounded.

For a while, people made a fuss over those who returned alive, and then people started to forget them.

"My friends at home stayed the same, but I came back a different person. I couldn't live as I had lived before, as they lived. And so I was left alone." Jack fell silent again, walked back and forth from one corner of the room to another, and sat down again on the edge of the table. How could I answer him? I felt uncomfortable around my old friends and I didn't have any new ones. When I met Seryoga, who had returned a year before I had because he was wounded, I hardly recognized him. He wasn't the Seryoga I remembered. It hurt me to see how much he had changed. A friend is always a friend; otherwise, he is not a friend at all. But I was lucky. I met Lyonka by chance. I didn't know him there, but we both had been in Afghanistan. In his eyes I saw exactly what I tried to hide in mine. Yes, I was really lucky.

"But not everyone was lucky. In a few years I began to dream about those who hadn't returned. I saw them in my dreams. I dreamed that I was returning to them." Jack fell silent again. It was late and he had to pack. He was going home to the States in the morning.

A month and a half later, some Moscow Afghantsi (whom I had met through Jack) called me in Leningrad and said that a second delegation of Vietnam veterans was coming. Lyonka took some comp time off work and, in a few hours, we were meeting them at the airport. They were about twenty years older than us, but we picked them out of the crowd at a glance. I don't even know why. Almost none of them spoke Russian, and only a few of us spoke English. Within five minutes we knew we had found friends, even more than that—blood brothers by blood. How did we understand each other? I don't know. But they understood us a lot better than our own people did. A big, strong American came up to us and asked for Vlad. I said, "Here I am," and stood in front of him. He stretched out his hand and said that Jack had entrusted him to me. It was John Messmore.

At that time, when I walked into the hotel, past the stately doormen, I didn't know that one day, along with some of my fellow Afghantsi, I would be standing with John at the Vietnam Wall in Washington, D.C., and that he would show me the names of his dead friends there. At that time, I explained to John that the dreary faces on our sidewalks were part of the Soviet local color, like the wooden *matryoshka* dolls. The people are not to blame. At that time I didn't know that Igor Zakharov and I would see for ourselves how advanced a prosthesis can be while we were in Seattle and how that would remind me of Kolka Tchuvanov and how he suffered with his peg leg. At that time, when I went with the Vietnamtsi to the "terribly secret" hospital for the disabled Afghantsi, I didn't know that in a year Kolka Knerick would come to an agreement with Jack for the production of modern wheelchairs. It was then that I first heard about post-traumatic stress disorder from John. I couldn't have imagined that I would ever sit across from thirty Vietnam veterans in a rehabilitation center near San Francisco. There I learned that Americans didn't just write dissertations on post-traumatic stress syndrome (as academicians do in my country), but that they treated people for it, too. At that time, I still didn't know anything.

"Did you know that the number of Vietnam veterans who have died from unnatural causes is already greater than the number of those who were killed in Vietnam?" I didn't know that, but after thinking about it, I answered by saying that this stress disorder wasn't a threat to me, that I wouldn't have to deal with it. "Just wait. It's still early," John said. "Your time will come." I burst out laughing and said, "Oh, no!"

But it's not funny anymore. Before, I tried to convince myself that if I hadn't been first to pull the trigger, then an Afghan would have remembered my eyes before my death instead of the other way around. And now? Now, I can't excuse myself, even in light of the fact that I, a nineteen-year-old boy, was flung into an alien land and forced to play a strange game of survival. Now, I can't use that excuse for having shot at them.

"Why do you have these meetings?" asked a reporter for the *New York Times*. "Because we don't want to see a new set of veterans of another war gather around this table fifteen years from now," I answered.

The interview came to an end. The reporter got up and shook hands with four of the veterans, two Afghantsi and two Vietnamtsi. He was ready to leave, but decided to come back. "Thank you," he said, "that was the best interview I have ever done."

This is me, in the first hours after I came back from Afghanistan. For 621 days, I dreamed about this day. And now I know what 621 days mean: 14,904 hours, 894,240 minutes.

And now I know that you can fall asleep with the thought that when you awaken, home will be eight hours closer.

And now I know that every evening you can cross off yet another day on the calendar, and just be happy that you are alive to do it.

And now I know the joy of crossing off the last day. Many didn't have the chance to know this joy.

There are two veterans in this picture. John Messmore, a Vietnam veteran, and Igor Zakharov, an Afghan veteran. Two veterans from different countries who came back from different wars at different times. But there's something they both share that unites them, and which others can't understand. When I come to Washington, D.C., John always meets me and I stay with him. "It's good that we met *here*," he told me once. "It's good that we didn't meet *there*."

I call this picture "VETERANS." It was taken on an airplane, somewhere between the United States and the Soviet Union.

ACKNOWLEDGMENTS

I would like to give special thanks to the following people from *USA Today* and Gannett News Service: Shawn Spense, Bill Perry, Susan Malone, Jaime Hennon, and Hollis Engley. Without their help and support I could not have produced this book.

Also my thanks to the following friends for the assistance they gave me with the book: Leonid Ivanov, Ekaterina Pomortsceva, John Messmore, Ken and Joanne Duvall, Paul Beals, Jerry Kiker, James Donaghe, Gordon Pavy, Narda Zacchino, Jose Olea, Sharon Tennison, Vladimir Shestakov, Mark Lazen, Jeff Chambers, Harrison Sheppard, Jack McDonald, Margarita Bekker, Diana Glasgow, Marianne Clarke Trangen, Dina Tamarova, and my parents, Inna and Evgenei Tamarov.

For their help with bringing this book back into print I would like to thank the following people who never lost faith and hope in me: my dear friend Christa Kodiak, my best friend Greg Williams, my agent Peter Beren, my assistant and friend Sandy Scheller, Dr. Mark Scheller, Vilen Golovko of the Flying Cranes, Inc., and last but certainly not least, Phil Wood at Ten Speed Press. Your kindness will always be appreciated.

VLADISLAV TAMAROV was a member of the Soviet Union's Airborne Assault Force and served on the front lines in Afghanistan as part of a minesweeping team. After the war, Tamarov worked as a professional break-dancer and mime for a year. Now he is a free-lance photographer, a writer, and an organizer of the Afghanistan Veterans. He lives in St. Petersburg.

NAOMI MARCUS received her master's degree from Columbia School of Journalism and has spent the last eight years as a free-lance journalist, translator, and interpreter. One of her favorite jobs was working with the Moscow Circus in California.

MARIANNE CLARKE TRANGEN has done interpreting and translating for commercial and nonprofit organizations. She interpreted in the PBS documentary "Brothers in Arms" about American veterans of Vietnam and Soviet veterans of Afghanistan.

Printed in the United States
by Baker & Taylor Publisher Services